POISON
FOR PROFIT

By

Mac B. McKinnon

EAKIN PRESS ꟼ Fort Worth, Texas
www.EakinPress.com

Copyright © 1992
By Mac B. McKinnon
Published By Eakin Press
An Imprint of Wild Horse Media Group
P.O. Box 331779
Fort Worth, Texas 76163
1-817-344-7036
www.EakinPress.com
ALL RIGHTS RESERVED
1 2 3 4 5 6 7 8 9
Paperback ISBN 978-1-68179-300-9
Hardback ISBN 978-1-68179-276-7
eBook ISBN 978-1-68179-278-1

Contents

I	Deep in the Heart of Texas	1
II	All the Right Stuff	5
III	Hard Work	11
IV	Contrasting Characters	19
V	Straight Talk	23
VI	Just Plain, Bad Luck	28
VII	New Victims	32
VIII	In Pursuit	37
IX	Nearing the End	41
X	The Cast of Characters	50
Photo Section		57
XI	Trial — Day 1	64
XII	Trial — Day 2	71
XIII	Trial — Day 3	79
XIV	Trial — Day 4	85
XV	Trial — Day 5	91
XVI	Trial — Day 6	96
XVII	Trial — The Final Day	101
XVIII	On to Llano	104
XIX	A Surprise	108
XX	In Summation	113
Epilogue		115

Preface

My dream over the years in journalism is to have a chance to follow a noted criminal case from beginning to end.

The case which is detailed in the following pages gave me just such a chance. By a stroke of fate, the case coincided with the sale of a weekly newspaper that I owned in Central Texas close to where part of the investigation was going on. My wife, Lea, first took note of the case and aroused my interest. Since that time, she has been instrumental in all the steps which took place toward finishing this work. It is for that reason that this book is dedicated to her.

Fortunately, I was acquainted with many of the people involved in the case because of my newspaper work so that gave me immediate credibility.

I could not have asked for a better case to write about as it involved many elements of mystery and an intensive investigation was necessary. Only when the trial unfolded did many pieces of the puzzle fall into place.

Expert after expert was called into the investigation both for the defense and prosecution, thereby making the case even more complicated and intriguing.

The results of all this landed a young man in jail for many years to come on a case that has set many legal precedents and the last has probably not been heard of this case in the halls of justice.

As far as circumstantial evidence goes, this case involving arsenic poisoning is probably one of the most bizarre to ever hit the courts of Texas.

It's also a case history on greed and what one man went through in his pursuit of success. It's not your usual profile of a serial killer as Timothy Glen Scoggin was loved and what he did was not for fun like other serial killers in the past few decades. It was purely cold-hearted and from all indications was fueled by greed in a relentless passion and pursuit of success.

Scoggin was a loner, like many other serial killers. But there the comparison with other serial killers ends. He was a fun-loving person who had a profession and many skills. But as one prosecutor said, he was as cold as ice and never once showed any remorse. Possibly the reason for no remorse, at least in Scoggin's mind, is that to this day he still maintains he is innocent of murder and attempted murder.

You be the judge.

Acknowledgments

There are simply too many people to name in expressing my appreciation for help in getting this book ready for publication.

Many people have gone out of their way to help and to everyone involved — you all know as well as I who you are — a great big, THANK YOU.

All sources of information are included within the text.

I hope I can at some time in the future return the favor.

CHAPTER I

Deep in the Heart of Texas

Texans have a certain image in this world. Timothy Glen Scoggin didn't fit this image with his 5-foot, 7-inch, 115 pound frame.

Residents of the Lone Star state are known to be bold, upfront individuals. Scoggin didn't fit this mold either. But he has a heart as bold and foreboding as any gunslinger who ever walked the streets of Texas.

There are two Texas towns involved in Scoggin's life, two towns now linked by sinister crimes unlike what might be expected out of the old west.

Llano, Texas, a town of 3,000 friendly folks and a few old soreheads, is full of robust, hearty individuals, the kind of people it took to carve a living out of this cedar-infested granite rock community.

The people here are much like the granite that lies just under the ground, peaking its gray and pink edges out of the dirt at regular intervals.

Over a period of thousands of years, the granite up thrust in and around Llano was covered by dirt blown in from the west by fabled West Texas sandstorms, a lot of which came from the Concho Valley.

In the heart of that valley sits the town of San Angelo. It's much the same as Llano except much larger with about 80,000 people. The character of the peoples of the two cities is much the same, a bunch of rugged individuals out of necessity due to the harsh nature of West Texas.

Linking the two towns is a ribbon of famed Texas highways stretching 130 miles. There's not much to be seen between the two cities. It's mostly cattle, sheep and goat country. San Angelo's claim to fame is being the sheep and goat capital of the world. There's a few other industries here and there including white gold (cotton) and black gold (oil).

There's little to see driving this stretch of road. There are only three towns, Brady, Eden, and Wall, a lot of cattle and fields of grain and cotton.

It had to be along this road that a wisp of a man, totally out of character in this tough country, hatched scheme after scheme to solve his financial woes. He obviously became more and more desperate as he sank in a quicksand of debt. Some people suspect that he didn't have debt problems but rather had an insatiable appetite for money. He once told a friend when asked what he wanted in this world that he wanted all the money in this world — every bit of it.

That man, Scoggin, impeccably dressed, was a man in a hurry to make it big. Like many a small man, he had trouble being taken seriously throughout his life. His high pitched voice and effeminate ways didn't earn him the respect of most Texans. Those endeared to him would fall victim to his greed.

Those targets were the elderly, usually the ones who didn't have anybody else and seemed to view him as a little boy who had not yet crossed the puberty line. Tim took friends where he could find them. Many thought him to be homosexual, with many a rumor behind that suspicion. It has been said that one of his male lovers died in Llano in the mid-1980s while another potential lover never responded to his advances and Scoggin had a broken heart when the man reconciled with his wife.

He cultured and nurtured the attention he got from the elderly. His hobby of china painting led him to the company of those who devoured his attentiveness. He was quite good at this hobby and had spent years developing his expertise. Scog-

2

gin made good money out of his hobby, a passion he enjoyed more than anything else in the world. In spite of his voluminous intake of coffee, his hands were as steady as those of a surgeon. He made gifts of many of his works to those around him.

It seems that Tim had his mind made up early in his life as to how he was going to make his fortune. In high school in Jal, New Mexico, his stated desire was to be a mortician like one of his relatives who had made it big in Oklahoma.

After being schooled in that field and entering the business, he quickly discovered that the only way to make money there was to own the funeral home. However, he did not waste the knowledge nor the acquaintances he made in that line of work.

Everybody knew him by Tim, which seemed to fit his little boy stature. Because of his hobbies, he always seemed to come in contact with the elderly who had money. It was for those people that Tim seemed to have limitless time. He came at their beck and call. He was young and impressionable and he was in awe of the good life that could be afforded with the money possessed by those he befriended.

He seemed to relish the idea of introducing those he knew to his other wealthy friends. He'd go out of his way. His plans were like those of an efficiency expert. He wasted little time or motion and covered a lot of ground in his young life.

Two of those people were Catherine "Girlie" Norton and Cordelia Norton, two spinster sisters, in Llano. He first met them when he was fresh out of mortuary school while he was serving an apprenticeship at Waldrope-Hatfield Funeral Home in Llano. In that role, he was in charge of taking care of floral arrangements for funerals. Girlie Norton owned the major florist in Llano and thus began a friendship.

The Norton sisters were the sole surviving members of a very well-to-do family in Llano with a history going back to the turn of the century. They were intelligent individuals with business acumen. They were their own persons. They were rich and lived in one of the few what could genuinely be called mansions in Llano. They were all the things that Tim Scoggin wanted to be. Most importantly, as it turned out, they had no heirs. They had what Tim Scoggin wanted — success, respect, and MONEY.

There were many others who helped Tim grease his skids to the desired goal of success and money and he used their acquaintances to the hilt. The Norton sisters helped him get a job in San Angelo, the others helped him get additional jobs and introduced him to the world of real estate and being an entrepreneur.

Two of those friends were Olgie and Leita Nobles, whom he met when he moved to San Angelo. They too had success, respect, and MONEY.

Many of those friends were escorted to Llano to meet the Norton sisters and to view their lavishly furnished mansion. He often told those around him that he would never have to worry about money as he was heir to a large estate.

It was in 1980 that he told one of those friends about an intriguing book he was reading. The book dealt with how a man used rat poison to kill people for their money. She thought the subject was grotesque and didn't pay much attention at the time. Little did that friend realize until eight years later the impact of that book on her young friend.

It wasn't beyond him to embroider on the truth to make an impression on someone. He was fond of telling people that he would never have to worry about money. He talked a lot about inheritance when the truth was that his family, although honest and hard working, were people of average means.

Statements of his own worth were greatly exaggerated. Much of what he had was ill gotten gains and the law still wonders where it is.

For some fourteen years, Tim Scoggin spun a web of deceit and greed. Then he got caught in it. The beginning of the end came quickly as Tim's financial house of cards came tumbling down about him. As he scrambled to get himself out of his web, he became even more entangled as one thing led to another and three people were dead, another escaped the death web and left Tim caught in the lurch.

The collapse of the web left Tim bankrupt, at least in a legal sense, and in jail serving a life sentence.

CHAPTER II

All the Right Stuff

Timothy Glen Scoggin started out in life with all the right stuff. He had a good family and the right kind of upbringing.

Born July 19, 1955 in Kermit, Texas, a small town in far West Texas with little on the horizon but oil drilling rigs, Tim led a life sheltered from the real world. He was the son his parents, Mackie and Billie, had always wanted. The senior Scoggin worked for El Paso Natural Gas, a company that was and is the predominant employer in much of West Texas and Eastern New Mexico.

It was in that scenario that Tim Scoggin was brought up — company towns — where there were no poor people, almost no blacks and few Mexicans. From Kermit, his family moved to Midkiff, then to Andrews and later to Jal, New Mexico.

It was in Andrews where the young man got his first taste of life. He became a born again Christian in the Baptist Church. He played pee-wee football and shortly before the age of thirteen, he earned the badge of Eagle Scout. It was not long after that when the family moved to Jal, New Mexico, just over the Texas border. Here there were no scouting programs but his father tried to get one started. After a year of effort, he gave up and Tim went on to other things. The young Scoggin apparently never forgot the Scouting motto, "Be Prepared."

Those other things amounted to a very active life. Taking art lessons, beginning with pencil and then oils, he became a very accomplished artist, continuing those painting endeavors up until the present time. He became an accomplished china painter which seemed to open many doors.

Tim has always been known to be an immaculate dresser and well groomed, almost to the point of being obsessed with it. Every wavy, auburn-colored hair was always in place. During high school, teachers noted that he worked hard to make money to spend on clothes. He was frugal with money, saving up to catch sales, mostly at what was known as the Model Shop in Odessa, some 100 miles from Jal.

Scoggin was a hard worker. It was said he must have worn out two or three lawn mowers taking care of yards in Jal during the summers. In school he learned photography and was sent to a school in Lubbock, Texas, on behalf of the school annual staff. Tim came back to Jal and used that knowledge to take pictures for the local newspaper and to take wedding pictures to earn extra money.

In high school, Tim was very active. He was on the student council all four years of high school, serving as parliamentarian of that group in his senior year. High School credits included playing in the band during the freshman and sophomore years. He was also a member of the annual staff for the last three years of high school. Senior class activities included participation in the drama club and holding the office of vice-president of that group. He attended workshops for the student council and as a photographer. In addition to being the artist for the annual his sophomore year and the annual photographer during the sophomore and junior years, he served as editor-in-chief of the annual staff in the final year of high school.

Kristi Scoggin, two years younger than her brother, was also on the annual staff.

As a student, he was just as hard a worker as in extracurricular activities. Not being the smartest of pupils, he tried hard and didn't mind asking for help, often doing extra work for additional credit. He had a particularly difficult time with science and math. The liberal arts such as English, accounting and typing came easier. Although there wasn't a speech impediment, he had a slight stammer, which one teacher believed was caused by his mind working faster than his mouth.

Tim was regarded as just a regular teenager in school, well balanced and normal. He was a member of what was thought of as a good class, the class of 1974, a group of about fifty students, many of whom still live in and around Jal.

It was well known that he had wanted to be a mortician since he was in junior high. His ambitions seemed strange to some of those who knew him back in Jal. He seemed too kind hearted for such an occupation, said one acquaintance while another didn't think Tim had what it took to be a mortician. Saving money toward that end, his conservative trends led him to buy a Ford Maverick before leaving Jal for Dallas, Texas, and mortuary school. He was also a very attentive person to those around him although he was often made fun of because of his small stature and effeminate ways.

His attentiveness was apparent to one teacher, Mollie Buffington, one of the student council sponsors, who sponsored a student trip to Europe after Tim's senior year. The trip lasted some six weeks and during that time included the date of Mrs. Buffington's wedding anniversary. Her husband, G. A., did not make the trip and for the first time in their long marriage they were not together on this special day. Tim boarded the tour bus in Europe with roses for her anniversary. He seemed to get more out of that trip than anyone else by being more attentive. He had worked hard to save money for the trip.

Following the trip, Tim returned to Jal for a short time before going to Dallas to attend the Dallas Institute of Mortuary Science with graduation coming a year later and then a job opportunity led to Llano.

After serving a year's apprenticeship at Waldrope-Hatfield Funeral Home in Llano, Tim Scoggin passed the test and received his funeral directors license on September 17, 1976. However, the Llano funeral home did not have an opening for another funeral director so it was time for Tim to move on. With the help of his new found friends in Llano, Cordelia and Catherine Norton, and a good recommendation from his employer, he was able to land a position at Massie Funeral Home in San Angelo.

San Angelo is like an oasis in the semi-arid region known as West Texas. It was in this setting that Tim Scoggin found new opportunities.

While in that position, he met a number of other people and made friends. Among those acquaintances were Irene and Jim Hutchins. Hutchins was a retired railroad man and was working in real estate investments. She was a secretary at the funeral home where Scoggin worked for almost two years, before leaving to become involved in other endeavors including real estate. In 1979, the Hutchins made him manager of one of their properties, Cactus Lane Mobile Home Park. Mrs. Hutchins introduced Tim to all her friends and many became fast friends, especially through his china painting hobby. Many of those around him were elderly and trusting. Some would rue the day that Tim Scoggin entered their lives.

Tim got his Texas Real Estate license on March 6, 1980. It was renewed in July 1987. He began to dabble in real estate. The Hutchins sold the trailer park in 1981 to a California corporation for $500,000. Tim stayed on as manager. He was quickly tagged as being uncommonly ambitious and those ambitions required money. The corporation found that money was missing from the trailer park and Tim finally fessed up to taking the money and reimbursed the company. He bought a house to be renovated and during that time there was a suspicious fire for which he received a very generous insurance settlement. A fire at a mobile home in the park drew the owners away from their business. While they were gone, a satchel of money at the business disappeared. The amount of money in the satchel was never disclosed.

During these years, Tim continued his friendship with the Norton sisters in Llano. He would often travel in a Lincoln Continental Town Car the 130 miles to that little town to visit and run errands. Often was the case, they would come to San Angelo to eat out or shop. Scoggin was right there to help.

In 1983, the Norton sisters discovered a safe, really nothing better than a lock box, was missing. In that safe was about $40,000 in cash, some fifty South African gold coins known as

Krugerrands and some stocks and bonds from the estate of the Norton sisters' father. There was no record of what the stocks were or their worth. About the same time, Scoggin rented a safe deposit box at a San Angelo bank. Some two years later, Scoggin listed among his assets the sale of $650,000 in stocks. In 1988, Scoggin sold thirty-five Krugerrands for $412 each to two Dallas coin dealers.

Attempts to investigate the missing safe from the Norton home were thwarted by the Norton sisters as they didn't want any of their friends to be bothered by it. This interference with the police and Texas Rangers came after the investigators told Girlie and Cordelia that there were no signs of forced entry and the theft appeared to be an inside job.

It was about this time that Jim Hutchins died followng a long illness. Tim was always there to comfort Irene Hutchins. During his illness, many days were spent at the famed Scott & White Hospital in Temple. Tim made numerous trips for them to take care of business. Irene turned to him more and more for advice. Following Jim's death, the talk turned to finances. She confided to Tim that she kept some Krugerrands in a lock box at the bank. He told her that was the worst thing she could do and that she should do as his parents had done — put the gold in a purse and hide it in the attic or some place safe at home. Although she had no intentions of doing what he suggested, she led him to think it was a good idea.

A few days later, she found out her young friend had paid a visit to her mobile home while she was away. He later told her he had stopped by to use the telephone. She knew he was lying.

His circle of acquaintances continued to grow, mostly elderly women with a few elderly men amongst them. There were a few younger ones, although much older than Tim. One of those was Jerldine Barrett, a fellow realtor, who later became a business partner. Their business venture was the purchase of a twelve-unit apartment house, known as Sagebrush Apartments. He introduced her to the Norton sisters and led her to believe he would never have to worry about money.

In 1984, Tim Scoggin returned to his old stomping

grounds, Jal, New Mexico, for his tenth year high school re-union. Said one classmate, who had regarded him as a loner and a nerd in high school, Tim came back as a wealthy person, at least that was what he wanted everyone to think. His financial web of deceit and greed was in its fledgling stages.

Tim Scoggin had a growing appetite for money.

CHAPTER III

Hard Work

To understand Catherine (Girlie) and Cordelia Norton, it is first necessary to understand their family.

Thomas William Norton and Mary Agnes Seggerson Norton were both from well to do families, he from Massachusetts and she from an area later to become the state of New Mexico. His family was in the granite business and he learned that particular trade at an early age. Her family was building a railroad across the Southwest. One of her brothers was killed doing that work by the famed Mexican bandit, Pancho Villa.

They met in San Antonio. He came there to work and she was attending school at the Catholic Our Lady of the Lake college. It wasn't long after they were married that he decided they would move to Llano, some 120 miles northeast of San Antonio to start the Llano granite works. He carved his fortune out of Llano's native granite, building one of the first granite processing plants in Texas and pioneering the development of the granite empire which gained for Llano the name, "Granite City." Norton was known as one of the finest granite carvers in the business.

The story goes, as told by Mrs. Norton to a reporter, that one day in 1900 soon after the young couple moved to Llano, they walked to the summit of a hill where construction of an imposing mansion was at a standstill.

Mrs. Norton was quoted as saying, "If I'm going to live in Llano, I'm going to live in this house!" To which, Tom Norton replied, "You're pretty ambitious aren't you? A nine-room house for two people?"

Sixteen years and five children later, the young man had amassed a considerable sum of money and the Norton family moved into that mansion, beginning what has been described as the opening chapter of an elegant legend which over a period of forty-five years became a tangible part of Llano's heritage.

The building had considerable history. Original construction began in 1863 by a Mr. Malone but halfway through the project, he ran out of money which might have been expected considering the materials out of which the building was being constructed and the nature of the construction.

The walls are of pressed brick, one-foot thick. Every room had a separate foundation of solid pink granite three-feet high. All of the wood in the house was cypress, imported from Liverpool, England. There were twenty-one hand-carved Doric galleries which nearly surrounded the mansion. There was enough wood in the gallery floors to build an average five-room house.

But in 1900, the Malone Mansion, as it became known, was bought for a proposed tuberculosis sanitarium and construction was resumed. In 1904, the Texas Sanitarium Center for Treatment of Tuberculosis opened its doors to the world.

The sanitarium was said to be one of the finest in the state. Around the headquarters building stood forty-four walled tents which housed the patients. On the breeze-swept galleries of the building, the patients could sit and enjoy the wide panorama which spread out in the valley below and extended as far across the hills as the eye could see.

However, shortage of funds forced the sanitarium to close its doors in 1908. In 1911, another attempt was made to operate the sanitarium but shortage of funds once again brought the venture to a halt.

In 1915, the building changed hands again as Norton purchased it and renovation began immediately. Almost two years later at the end of 1916, the Norton family moved in, a sixteen-year-old dream realized by Mrs. Norton. In the years that followed, the Nortons were occupied with rearing their family of five girls, which they did in regal fashion. There was a host of hired help including a seamstress to sew the girls' school clothes, a cook, a house cleaner and a gardener.

The home was said to be a beehive of activity and the scene of many social gatherings. However, while all this may sound like a dream, things were not that easy for the Norton family.

On their arrival in Llano, they had a number of things against them. Tom and Agnes were both very independent and what might be called hot-headed. They never hesitated to speak their piece.

They were considered outsiders with Tom being a Yankee. They were Republicans and there were only about five families of those in this Democratic country at the time. To this day, Republicans are considered suspect in Llano.

In addition, the Nortons were anti-prohibitionist and at that time, this attitude was scandalous. To top it off, they were Catholics and few, if any white folks, in the entire area were of that religion.

There wasn't even a Catholic Church in town at the time but the Nortons soon helped to solve that situation. The temperaments of the parents were passed on to the daughters. All were known to be willing to fight at the drop of a hat, especially the next to the eldest, Cordelia, and they could hold their own with fists or words with any man.

Their daughters were Polly, born in 1902; Cordelia, born in 1904; Eleanor, whose birth date was 1906; Margaurite came along in 1908 and Catherine (Girlie) four years later in 1912.

The father saw to it that all the girls received a good education and all but Margaurite attended and were graduated from the University of Texas at Austin, some seventy miles east of Llano.

Perhaps because of their differences with the rest of the community, the Nortons were very private people. Some of their disputes came to actual blows. At one time, Tom Norton was accused of having shot a deer out of season. He was found guilty by a jury and had to pay a hefty fine. A short time later, he was in the Post Office and someone asked how the trial went. To this, Tom replied that the "son-of-a-bitches" got me. It so happened that on the other side of the wall was one of the jurors who took offense to being called a son-of-a-bitch and came round the corner to confront Norton. He asked Tom if he was talking about him? "Damn right I was," Norton replied and they promptly went to fist city. There are no accounts of who won the fight.

Mrs. Norton was known to express her feelings a number of times in words not considered acceptable for a lady to speak. Those mannerisms were also a part of the five daughters' lives as well.

In spite of all this or perhaps because of it, there was never known to be a fight within the family. The father, a portly, barrel-chested man, was the king of the house and his petite wife, the queen. For instance, although all the girls smoked after they became adults, none did so at home or in the presence of their parents, as that was the rule of their father.

Even though they weren't necessarily well liked in the community, they were respected. It was known that the Nortons would help anybody down on their luck. But they didn't want anyone to know about their generosity.

Stories of their generosity are endless as almost everyone has something to relate but they know nothing about how the Nortons may have helped others, only their own individual stories.

Their openness and honesty, although at times taking crude forms, won them respect in the community. It was accepted that the whole family relationship was different. They had a set of values that didn't coincide with others. Why, it was known that they voted for Herbert Hoover.

Even though they had a lavish lifestyle, the Nortons felt the crunch of the depression in the 1930's like everyone else. They still had the best car in town, usually a convertible, and entertained lavishly. Tom would scream about all the expenses. Then he'd have to do things like fix up special granite grave sidings at the cemetery to settle debts. The bills continued to pile up.

When Polly finished college, she went off to work for the government in Washington, D.C. Eleanor, who was teaching school, started a florist business in Llano during the 1930's and Catherine went to school in Houston to learn more about the florist business.

Then in 1940, Cordelia, who worked on occasions as a gas station attendant, became one of the first distributors for Lone Star Beer and quickly took the distributorship from nothing to number one in the market. At first, her distributorship covered Llano County only, but was later expanded to include neighboring Burnet and Lampasas counties.

It was thought that the beer distributorship was what pulled the Norton family out of debt. With the advent of World War II, the granite business, which was already suffering from economic woes due to the depression, really went to nothing.

In tough times, the family became even closer. With the beginning of the war, Cordelia and Eleanor became commissioned officers in the Women's Army Corps. Cordelia enlisted in January 1943 and was sent to nurses school in Springfield, Missouri. Medicine was one of her first loves as she had intended to be a doctor but learned she had to study Latin. That was the end of that plan. However, her military service was short as she was discharged in August 1943 when a heart condition she had suffered from since childhood was discovered.

The heart disorder was supposed to have kept her from becoming an adult, but as she proved all her life, she was tough. Disappointed in not being able to serve in the military, she returned home to run the beer distributorship which had been run by Margaurite during her absence.

Eleanor was also a commissioned officer and served from June 30, 1943, until June 23, 1945, being promoted to first lieutenant before she was discharged from her duties as passenger and freight transportation officer at Ogden Air Field in Utah. She made many friends during that time, friends who would be invited to Llano from all over the world and entertained lavishly.

During all these years, the Nortons spent a handsome fortune decorating their mansion. The mansion was remodeled to have thirteen rooms and houses a fabulous collection of antiques, some of which are so valuable it would be practically impossible to evaluate them. Several fortunes are said to be represented in these antiques, which range from delicate crystal to ancient bronze statues of Columbus and Queen Isabella.

One reporter wrote of a tour of the home, saying, "Recently (1961), I visited the Nortons for this story and I shall never forget what I saw that day. As I walked across the plush carpets, I was struck by the magnificent beauty of the sitting room which opened off the entry way. It was like viewing a forgotten era.

"In one end of the room there was an ornately-carved Mathushek piano, more than one hundred years old. Some of the many other valuable antiques include two ornate chairs from the Vatican in Rome, a Chinese urn more than two hundred years old, a rose Venetian glass chalice with gold design reputed to be the only one of its kinds in existence, an Indian-print nine-by-twelve tapestry, "Tree of Life," which came from India and is over one hundred years old . . . at the other end of the room, an Italian-imported library table, ornately carved and complete with concealed compartments.

"Before I left, Mrs. Norton showed me a part of her elephant collection. Collected from all parts of the world, the elephants are unique in as much as each of them is carved with upturned trunks. Down-turned trunks bring bad luck, Mrs. Norton said. The elephants range in size from no larger than a thumb nail to about two feet and are carved out of such materials as crystal, ivory, jade, ebony, and alabaster."

As good as all this might seem, it was real life and apparently too good to last. A tragic end to what was once a happy family began to unfold. Tom Norton developed cirrhosis of the liver due to his heavy drinking. He died on February 5, 1948, at the age of eighty-one. Some say he died at work while the death certificate shows he died at home. There were thoughts that he may have had cancer that hastened his death and an illness that was to afflict the rest of the family in the not-to-distant future.

It was said by family friends that Norton was more revered by his family in death than he had been while alive.

Norton's death had a dramatic effect on his family. The five sisters made a pact they would never marry. Mrs. Norton took over ruling the family roost, although Cordelia actually did the man's job of wearing the pants in the family, both literally and figuratively.

Six years later, Eleanor died in the nearby San Saba hospital after a five month bout with ovarian cancer. Few people in Llano even knew she was sick. Funeral arrangements were made by a San Saba funeral home as the Nortons, always faithful to Llano businesses, had gotten upset with the Llano funeral home due to a good friend of theirs being dismissed.

Before Eleanor's death, Polly had come home from Washington, D.C., to die. She had been suffering from breast cancer for fifteen years but late in 1953, she could no longer fight it off and came home. She died a month and a few days after Eleanor, on April 12, 1954. Death came at home. Few people in Llano knew of her illness or even that she had come home.

At that time, Llano did not have a hospital, only a clinic. In the next few years, the three remaining Norton sisters and Mrs. Norton worked to get a hospital in their town, an effort that was successful in the late 1950s.

However, when Mrs. Norton became ill with rectal cancer she was referred to a San Antonio hospital. She died on October 20, 1962, two months after it was learned she had cancer.

The funeral for Mrs. Norton was something that people in Llano still remember. For one thing, it was one of the few times they had ever seen Cordelia in a dress. She told friends she would have worn slacks if the priest would have allowed it. The funeral was held in the Catholic Church that the Norton's so generously supported. The wreath done by her daughters was spectacular with the casket covered in a spray of camellias.

Margaurite was the second mother in the home. She didn't go to college as did her sisters and she rarely worked in family businesses, only to fill in. She helped run the mansion.

Margaurite probably suffered the most of any of the family as she had cancer, first detected in the breast, for four years and five months before her death on February 10, 1965, in a Llano Nursing Home.

Margaurite's funeral was held in the mansion, conducted by Edgar Funeral Home in Burnet. The owners of the funeral home, a married couple, spent several nights in the Norton Mansion at the insistence of Cordelia. This led to joking that Tom Norton would turn over in his grave if he knew a man other than himself was spending the night under that roof. The funeral for Margaurite was conducted by an Episcopal priest. The family had had a falling out with the Catholic Church.

Now, Catherine and Cordelia were alone in the big house on the hill.

CHAPTER IV

Contrasting Characters

Catherine Norton was the smallest of the Norton sisters. Although all the sisters were slender, they were rather tall for women of their era, standing five-foot six or seven inches. Catherine was shorter, somewhat like her mother.

Because of this and her feminine ways, such as always wearing a hat and gloves and frilly clothes, she was nick-named "Girlie" in early childhood. Some of her close friends in later years thought this to be inappropriate as she was such a lady and they would not use the nickname.

Unlike her sister Cordelia, Catherine never wore pants. She was always the picture of propriety.

She was also the most public of the Nortons, working in the flower shop she owned and then later adding a dress shop that became one of the best known in the area for its quality. One of its trademarks was Catherine's service and attention to detail. She never forgot a name or a size. She also knew the economic means of her clients and often reduced prices to fit the budget of her customers.

She was known as a tough competitor but being in the clothes business did not come easily. It was different than flowers, a business she knew very well and had no trouble learning and dealing with.

The dress shop came into being when Catherine built new facilities for the florist business on Highway 29 on the West Side of Llano in the late 1950s. She handled medium to better price women's clothes. A competitor said she was a good retailer but not a good buyer. She couldn't balance her buying. Realizing she had a problem, she secured the services of a management consultant in Dallas who taught her how to buy so she could start making money. She was said to be good at seeking and taking advice on running the business.

Catherine and Cordelia continued their lavish lifestyle following Margaurite's death, a way of living they had enjoyed all of their lives. They went first class on everything. However, Catherine was the only one who did extensive travelling, most of it through associations with florists. She travelled all over the world, collecting valuable articles for use in decorating the home.

She was proud to display an autographed picture of Pope John in the home, an article she had obtained after a papal audience at the Vatican on one of her trips.

On these trips, she made many friends. She would later visit them, many of whom lived in other countries. They in turn would come to Llano to visit her and were lavishly entertained.

During Catherine's world jaunts, trips that her mother had accompanied her on during her lifetime, Cordelia and an employee/friend, Annie Lottie Wykcoff, who was a widow, would travel about Texas, shopping and going to sporting events. The Nortons loved sports. In earlier years, they would attend all Llano high school sporting events and then later only the home games. They held season tickets for Llano sports.

They would play host to graduating girls at a teen hangout operated by Wycoff and all seniors would get gifts from the Nortons.

Many of the parties in the home centered on sports such as Super Bowl parties. There were also Christmas parties with the Nortons exchanging gifts with many people. There were Easter Egg hunts at the home but only for adults. Children were seldom if ever in attendance at the home.

The sisters, Catherine and Cordelia, fit in well with people and always were surrounded with people, mostly couples of solid financial means. While they were outspoken people with strong beliefs, they did not thrust those opinions or beliefs on people and would do so only if asked. When these parties were held before Mrs. Norton's death, she would stay in her bedroom.

Catherine, whose bedroom was upstairs and called the lookout for some unknown reason, loved to cook, but her concoctions always left many people wondering what they had eaten. She collected cook books from all over the world and she was fond of always trying something different, either from a cookbook or recipes on the side of ingredient boxes. Whatever she tried didn't always turn out real good. Cordelia was fond of chiding her baby sister about her cooking failures.

Catherine was probably better known for the things she did for other people because she was the more public member of the family and she was more in the public's eye due to the nature of her businesses. She would never talk about the favors she did but other people didn't hesitate to talk.

She once sold a dress to a lady, Betty Berry, head dispatcher for the Llano County Sheriff's department. The day after buying the dress, Berry and her husband went fishing and while they were gone, their home burned. A few days later, Catherine showed up at the door of their temporary residence with a sack of clothes. When asked about it, Catherine replied that since Mrs. Berry hadn't gotten to wear the clothes she bought, it was only fair that her dress shop replace them.

Another friend who worked for Catherine at times doing various chores, was divorced. Catherine asked what she was going to do when her ex-husband got remarried. The woman replied that she was going to celebrate.

When that day came, the woman found a bottle of champagne in her refrigerator with a pink bow on it. Catherine had placed it there when she came to the woman's house to deliver some flowers for another occasion.

Catherine was known to be an astute business woman and made a number of investments. One of those investments was in 1933 when she bought fifty gold South African Krugerrands from T. D. (Dutch) Swenson, a Llano businessman and coin dealer.

It was those coins that were stolen from the Norton home in 1983. It was those coins that led the law to a Norton friend, Tim Scoggin. Tim and Catherine had become friends during the 1970s when he was an apprentice funeral director at the Waldrope-Hatfield Funeral Home in Llano.

For some reason, and no one seems to know or imagine why, Tim and Catherine became good friends. She invited Tim into her home. Tim obviously ate up the attention he was getting from a well-known, respected rich person in Llano society and he relished the attention. He spent every spare minute with Catherine and got to know Cordelia as well. It was an odd friendship as the Norton sisters usually socialized with friends near their own age and usually only couples. Scoggin served as a chauffeur to the two ladies as he escorted them around Llano, San Angelo, and other points in Texas.

When it came time for him to leave Llano at the end of his apprenticeship, the Nortons were helpful in getting him another position, this time with a funeral home in San Angelo.

This gave Tim access to more people who would figure in his future. But he did not forget Catherine and Cordelia Norton. He would be there when both died, a day apart.

CHAPTER V

Straight Talk

Cordelia Norton was the son Tom Norton never had. From day one, she dressed and acted like a man in a rough and tumble man's world.

She would fight at the flip of an eyelash, curse like a sailor and tell the dirtiest jokes. And she could tell them better than anyone else could.

But she was a girl at heart. She had an extensive doll collection that she liked to spend time with. And that girlish heart was made of pure gold, although it appeared to be iron from the outside. Even in her childhood when a friend, Jim Inks, was stricken with a disease that kept him at home for an extended period, Cordelia came by with a Hershey candy bar every day.

She was known to help many friends of her mother's even after Mrs. Norton died. Her civic endeavors were many, although a well guarded secret, known only by those closely involved in whatever effort she was helping.

When schools in Llano County were consolidated, one prominent landowner would not pay taxes for several years, causing a bit of a financial crunch for the schools. He said he didn't have any children so he shouldn't have to pay taxes.

In a public meeting, Cordelia so humiliated the man that

he paid the taxes on the spot. It was said that few lawyers did as much legal work as Cordelia.

She threw a big party when the Llano swimming pool first opened in the fifties, having a group of Lone Star Beer performers come to Llano and then invited many friends to her home for a cook-out, prepared by a family friend, Tab Summers of San Angelo, formerly of Llano.

She was also a very loyal person to those she chose to befriend. One such instance was Tab Summers who at one time worked for Waldrope-Hatfield Funeral Home in Llano. After Summers got what Cordelia considered to be a raw deal, she would no longer have any business dealings with the funeral home although she and its owners remained friends.

While not loved by everyone, she was respected, not only for her position in the community and her business abilities but for being honest and direct. Cordelia either liked you or she didn't. There was no in-between. Her kind side was demonstrated by the well known fact that every stray animal was welcome at the Norton home. Cordelia would take them in and feed them so well that she would get strong words from the veterinarian. Many of those pets had to be put on a diet because of her lavish feeding habits.

All pets were treated well and lived there until they died or were provided with a new home. There is an extensive pet cemetery near the Norton Mansion, with each pet having a granite head stone. She was known to stop along the road and pick up stray animals.

Jimmy Lee Ward, a black man who worked for Cordelia from time to time — those times being dictated by whether or not she was mad at him — noted that Cordelia always had a black cat. At one time she had three, one named Martin, another was Luther and the third was named King.

Ward was employed mostly to help Cordelia take care of two herds of Black Angus cattle, bred with the finest of registered Angus bulls kept in a barn behind the Norton Mansion on the seventy-acre estate.

Although she didn't keep papers on the cattle, she knew them all by name and on Sunday mornings, she would ride out with Ward to feed the cattle and make a count. The keeping of cattle followed her father's example of always having cattle herds.

One lease had about forty head of cattle in a community known as Lone Grove and another hundred head on a lease at Oxford, south of Llano.

She knew how to have a good time but she was always a business person first. She and Catherine were known to go with a group of friends to "bar-hop" in taverns around a neighboring lake, Lake Buchanan, the first lake in a string of lakes known as the Highland Lakes of Texas on the Colorado River. She would always buy anybody in the bars a Lone Star Beer.

She also knew how to throw a party. Everybody who was somebody got invited. And when they had a party, the Norton sisters did all the cooking. Cordelia cooked most of the time and her food was the staple of life, very plain and to the point, just like she was. As one friend said, it was food you could eat that would stick with you when you dug a post hole.

That was the kind of food she needed for the hard work she did. She was known to be on her beer trucks every day. Later in the 1950s, she hired a young man, Jim Myers, who would later take over the distributorship. Myers was a good worker who had Cordelia's confidence. He took over the distributorship several years before her death although she was active in the business until the end.

The Nortons worked a good many people. They paid well but they expected quality work. If a person worked anywhere around the house, they took meals with the Nortons. After Mrs. Norton died, Cordelia ran the household. She paid the bills and made the purchases, including the Cadillacs they drove. She made sure the family's cemetery plot was always taken care of.

All members of the family are buried in the plot with St. Augustine grass and a sprinkler system. It was kept in an immaculate condition. The headstones were simple with each family name, year of birth and death and a cross. Also buried in that plot is a woman referred to as Aunt Cliney. She was not actually related but worked for the Nortons and became more than just an employee. She apparently had no other family. When she died in 1951, she was included in the family plot. Her grave marker reads Annie David Clinefelter, 1867–1951.

Cordelia was proud of the family mansion. Open houses were held frequently, especially if some organization needed to raise money by selling tickets for home tours. The big open house came in 1976 during the bicentennial of the United States. There were many others.

Anyone who insulted her home would incur her wrath. A very close friend of many years once told her when she was re-doing the cypress wooded front veranda that she should just pour concrete. She didn't speak to him for months. She found her cypress in Louisiana and acquired it at considerable cost.

The upkeep on the old mansion was expensive. In the late 1960s she had the building sandblasted and had to hire extra help for several months to clean up after the project. An interior decorating firm came in from Austin and re-did the entire home, including drapes and much of the carpeting. One thing that was not touched, however, was Mrs. Norton's bedroom. It, with a beautiful black bedroom suite, was left just as it was when Mrs. Norton died. Her hair brush remained on the dresser exactly as she had left it. The room was only entered for cleaning purposes.

Although she never was married or had children and children were never an integral part of her life, Cordelia had a soft spot for youngsters. It was thought she and Catherine had a number of children overseas that they sponsored. One picture of a child with her letter of thanks had a prominent spot in the home.

Her attire often caused rumors about Cordelia, rumors about her sexual preferences. However, no one would speak anything out of the ordinary about her. It was thought she dressed that way because of her work and because she believed she was the son her father wanted. And any man would have been proud to dress as well as she did with tailored suits, oxford shoes and always a tie, sometimes with a hat. She always paid for things in cash out of her back pocket, just like a man.

Everything about Cordelia made people wonder how a

person such as Tim Scoggin could have worked his way into her life. Although he was ambitious and an apparent hard worker, there was nothing else the two had in common. But after being introduced to Cordelia by Catherine, all three became constant companions.

He came at their beck and call and everyone wondered how Scoggin could afford so much time from his job and businesses to take care of the Nortons. His motives later became apparent.

CHAPTER VI

Just Plain, Bad Luck

Good health was something the Norton family was not blessed with. Being the kind of people they were, they tried to make the best of what they were given. A prime example of that came in the 1970s after the mandatory seat belt law went into effect.

Cordelia came into contact with the then county attorney for Llano, L. T. DesChamps, and the attorney of record for the Norton estate. She told him with a shake of her forefinger in his face that she was not going to wear a seat belt.

He replied to her that in Llano it probably wouldn't matter because it wouldn't be enforced that rigidly. But, in other areas she would be given a ticket. That is, unless she could get some kind of an exemption from a doctor.

To this, Cordelia replied that since she had a pacemaker, she could probably get just such an exemption. Several days later as he was driving down the street, DesChamps passed her and she waved a piece of paper at him to prove she had gotten the exemption from wearing a seat belt.

Cordelia suffered a heart disorder from early childhood. It was a disorder that the family was told would not allow her to live to become an adult. As in many cases, she proved everybody wrong and lived to an age that surpassed everyone in the family.

However, she did apparently escape the dreaded cancer that afflicted her sisters, mother, and possibly her father. Catherine developed cancer and had both breasts removed a number of years before her death. In addition, she was suffering from heart disease. Only a few months before her death, she had undergone surgery for cancer of the pancreas.

Due to their age, Cordelia and Catherine had begun to slow down in the 1980s. They required more help from people they employed as well as friends, friends such as Tim Scoggin. In about the last six months of their lives, neither felt well and complained about having stomach pains.

Those pains and accompanying vomiting and dysentery seemed to coincide with visits to the home by Scoggin.

In November 1987, Dr. Dan Hoerster of Llano, Cordelia's doctor for some twenty years, treated her for hallucinations, vomiting and diarrhea. He thought it was a virus.

In January 1988, Cordelia fell and broke her shoulder coming down the back steps of the mansion.

Jeanette McPherson, a nurse at the Llano hospital, had been staying at the Norton mansion about two and a half months taking care of Cordelia. She stayed there most of the time with Scoggin staying the times she was unable to do so.

On Monday before the sisters died at the end of the week, Cordelia became even more ill than before. Dr. Hoerster gave her additional medicine. This didn't help. She was admitted to the hospital on Thursday, February 18. During this week, Scoggin drove Catherine to the famed Scott & White Clinic in Temple, some 180 miles away for a checkup on her earlier cancer surgery. She passed the checkup with flying colors. Tim brought her home on Thursday, February 18 and the next morning, he found her dead. Doctors at Scott & White were shocked.

The official cause of death was listed as heart failure. She was seventy-five. Tim took care of matters at the house and made funeral arrangements, calling the family attorney, Mary Moursund DesChamps and writing checks with Cordelia's name on them to pay household help.

Tim visited Cordelia in the hospital every day. The day after Catherine died, Cordelia died in the Llano hospital. The

29

official cause of death was listed as pneumonia which brought about congestive heart failure. She was eighty-three. Scoggin moved quickly, calling Edgar Funeral Home in Burnet to arrange cremation of the bodies and burial of the ashes.

He notified the attorney again. The day following Cordelia's death, Tim and the attorney fixed a meal for everyone in the home, then Tim called everyone into the living room and asked them to leave as the will was going to be read and only he, the attorney and family friend Nell Summers, were to be present.

However, Mrs. DesChamps (who normally uses her maiden name for business reasons due to the fame of her father, A. W. Moursund, a political protege of President Lyndon B. Johnson and because she began her career under that name) informed Scoggin that the will could not be read until it was filed for probate.

In the meantime, the attorney asked Scoggin and Summers to list assets of the estate since they seemed to know so much about the business dealings of the Norton sisters.

Mary Moursund DesChamps was the executress of the estate and signed forms to authorize cremation of the bodies. It seemed strange to everyone in the community that the bodies were to be cremated.

The Norton family had always been supportive of the city cemetery and none of the other family members were cremated. However, Scoggin was accepted on his word that Catherine and Cordelia had wished their remains to be cremated. No one in the community thought it strange that the two sisters died within a day of each other. It was known that both were in failing health and due to their ages, no one gave it a second thought.

The cremated remains of the sisters in urns were laid to rest in the family plot in the Llano City Cemetery on February 22 in graveside services. A Catholic priest recited last rites with a large crowd of friends on hand.

On February 25, the will was filed for probate and the attorney informed Scoggin and Summers of the contents. Neither was named as a beneficiary, rather the estate was split between trusts to be established to benefit the cemetery association and Robinson Llano City Park. The only exception was a tract of land given to a long time friend.

Tim was shocked and totally silent when told the contents of the will. This was totally unlike his previous behavior. He had told a number of friends he was in line for a big inheritance, possibly as much as a million dollars to be split with another person and that he never had to worry about money.

He supposedly needed the money as he was allegedly deeply in debt at the time. Some thirty days later, the Norton family attorney discovered Scoggin had helped himself to $30,000 from the Nortons by writing a check on the estate, cashed after the deaths. He told the attorney he was in financial trouble and Catherine agreed to loan the money to him.

He later claimed the Norton sisters gave him the $30,000 for his help in their times of need.

The time of need was actually Scoggin's and his need became even more desperate when he learned he was not an heir to the Norton estate which was valued at more than five million.

It wasn't until later that year that it was discovered that Cordelia Norton died of arsenic poisoning, a poison that had been administered to her over a period of several months.

It is believed that Catherine Norton died after being administered strychnine, the reason she went so quickly after having been given a clean bill of health by doctors.

CHAPTER VII

New Victims

Olgie Nobles was born February 25, 1917 in Central Texas, the oldest of four boys. He grew up in the Dublin-Hico-Clariette area of Central Texas and was almost a grown man when his family moved in 1935 to Lampasas, not far from the Texas state capitol of Austin.

Nobles was involved in the trucking business and it was through this enterprise that he met his future wife, Leita Sutton. She was one of nine children raised on a tenant farm near Lampasas. They were married August 10, 1942, his first marriage and her second. She had a son, Pharis (Butch) James by the first marriage.

Olgie and Leita never had children, instead having to concentrate on taking care of Butch who was a severe diabetic, who later became almost blind and lost both legs to amputation.

Olgie drove a cattle truck in the spring and summer and worked in the fall and winter for Leita's brother, Leonard, buying and selling furs, pecans, eggs, and scrap metal.

Olgie and Leita set up their own business in San Angelo in 1962 when they bought a group of concrete-block buildings on the Rio Concho River.

In the spring and summer, they sold, installed and serviced evaporative coolers — known by the common name of swamp boxes. In the fall and winter, they reverted to buying and selling pecans and furs.

The business had grown and prospered over the years as the Nobles were frugal. Both worked in the business with Olgie being known to keep money stashed away in various places so that Leita wouldn't know about it.

It was a stormy relationship at best with Olgie having a taste for the grape and an eye for the girls. Leita was stern and business like. More than one person described them as fighting like cats and dogs.

They lived in the Cactus Lane Trailer Park. It was there that they got to know Tim Scoggin. They fell under his spell. Scoggin managed the trailer park although he was known to tell people he owned it.

On one occasion, the Nobles' trailer home caught fire through mysterious circumstances. They were called to the scene. During their absence from the business, a satchel full of money left at the air conditioning firm disappeared. It was never known what happened to it and no one has ever said how much money it contained, but it was known to be substantial.

For some reason, the Nobles were a pushover for Scoggin, especially Olgie. Any time he needed money, he went to Olgie and on nothing more than a handshake, the money was his.

One such instance came when Scoggin got caught dipping his hand in the till at the trailer park. He had told some people he was going to borrow the money from a bank to reimburse the California owners but he did get $34,000 from the Nobles, telling them he had to have it to keep a bank from seizing "his" trailer park.

After the fire, the Nobles moved into a home in the Grape Creek area just outside of San Angelo.

All during this time, the friendship between Scoggin and the Nobles was growing.

In 1985, while Leita was vacationing in Las Vegas, Scoggin persuaded Oglie to sell him the air conditioning business and buildings.

The deal was closed on September 25, 1986, with the bank financing $49,000 of the deal and the Nobles carrying a note for $80,000 which was to be paid off at the rate of $1,700 per month.

On October 3, just eight days later, a release of lien was filed at the Tom Green County Courthouse showing that Scoggin paid off the $80,000. The Nobles didn't know of this and it was later shown that their signatures were forged. Some six months later, Scoggin used the release of lien to secure another bank loan.

All the while, Scoggin paid the Nobles monthly or at least he satisfied them that he was trying to make the payments. Leita worked at the business to help him learn the ropes. She worked for nothing. Against her advice, he stopped handling furs and pecans. He added a line of hardware against Leita's advice. He remodeled the buildings, also against Leita's advice. Leita knew that things weren't going well as she was there when people tried to collect money from Scoggin. She had to handle the situation for him.

He decided to add a specialty store called Addie Mae's Christmas and More store, which mainly was seasonal, specializing in Christmas decorations. Olgie loaned him $20,000 to finance this new venture.

After selling out to Scoggin, Olgie retired and spent his time puttering around the house, mainly in a private room at the rear of the house, drinking and smoking. Neighbors reported that Scoggin came by often to visit with Olgie.

Throughout this time span, Scoggin was a very busy, little man. Not only was he a devoted son to his parents, now retired and living in Midland, but he attended to every need of the Nobles and made regular trips to Llano to visit the Norton sisters.

On top of all this, he entertained the Norton sisters every time they came to San Angelo, lavishing attention on them and their every need. The Norton sisters were known to telephone the air conditioning business regularly.

Leita reported she had begun to recognize their voices. She recalled a particular conversation — she only heard Scoggin's side of it — but he said something about needing poison to kill coyotes on Cordelia Norton's ranch. Leita also remembered that John Poss, a subcontractor who installed coolers

34

for the Nobles, had a permit to buy strychnine and offered to get some for Scoggin from a dentist he knew who raised cattle.

The conversation was indeed strange as Llano ranchers have few problems with coyotes. However, it was later alleged that Catherine Norton died of strychnine poisoning but it was never proven.

On the morning of December 21, 1987, while making a regular run to a liquor store, Olgie collided his pickup with a truck. Witnesses said it appeared he was sightseeing.

He suffered severe facial injuries and doctors had to completely reconstruct his face. This required that his diet consisted of nothing but baby food. Leita had to quit helping Scoggin to take care of Olgie.

While taking care of Olgie, she was not feeling well herself, suffering from ulcers that were bleeding and she developed a bad, constant case of diarrhea. She lived on 7-Up and stomach relief medicines such as Maalox and Riopan-Plus.

Scoggin was constantly serving their every need, bringing the mail, groceries and medicine.

As the days lengthened into weeks and the weeks into months, it appeared that Olgie was getting better. But then Leita came home one morning to find him violently ill with severe stomach cramps, diarrhea and vomiting. Although he had been suffering from complications of the accident, this appeared to be a different ailment. Leita wanted to take him to the hospital but Olgie would have nothing to do with it. On the morning of the fourth day, March 27, 1988, Olgie was dead, five weeks after the deaths of the Norton sisters.

The first person Leita called was Scoggin who was visiting his parents in Midland. He was Johnny on the spot, helping out with Leita's every need and a few days after the funeral, he came by to help address thank-you notes.

Two days after Olgie's death, a check on his account dated three days before the death in the amount of $15,000 was deposited into Scoggin's bank account.

Leita continued to get sicker and sicker. In May, Scoggin drove her to Brownwood where a doctor diagnosed her problem as bleeding ulcers. She was admitted to the hospital and given blood transfusions.

Scoggin visited her and checked on her constantly. Following her two-week confinement, Scoggin drove her home. Within a week she was worse and on May 28 Leita was admitted to Shannon Memorial Hospital in San Angelo with severe stomach cramps, diarrhea and vomiting and in a paralyzed condition. Doctors ran test after test trying to determine the problem.

While in the hospital, Leita was notified by her bank that five checks with suspicious signatures had been written on her account. The checks totalled $38,700 and were deposited into Scoggin's account.

Then the test results were conclusive. Leita was a victim of arsenic poisoning. The poison, tests showed, had been administered to her over a period of time.

The person who tried to kill Leita Nobles did not have a full understanding of how arsenic works in the human body. Although it disappears from the blood system in no longer than four days, it is a heavy metal and can be found in the hair, fingernails and toenails indefinitely. The person also apparently didn't realize that given in too small a dose, a person's system can build up a tolerance.

If given as little as a gram, victims will usually die anywhere from twenty-four to seventy-two hours later after experiencing vomiting, diarrhea, stomach cramps and convulsions.

Tests on Leita Nobles showed she had at first been given a very small dose. Testing her hair, lab specialists could read the strands like rings of a tree to determine how big a dosage of arsenic she had been given. The first dose was only 8.5 parts per million while the one that put her into paralysis and in Shannon Memorial Center registered a whopping 130.1 parts per million, a dose that would normally have been fatal except that Leita's system had built up a tolerance.

Tests on Olgie's remains showed that he died from a dose of 99.8 parts per million. For the killer, the small doses for Leita brought about an investigation that normally wouldn't have ever occurred if she had died. It probably would have been written off as a death of another elderly woman due to natural causes.

The man with the key to unlock this puzzle was Leita's nephew, a man who had gained a national reputation for his abilities at prosecution. Ron Sutton went to work on the case.

CHAPTER VIII

In Pursuit

Ronald L. Sutton is a bulldog of a man — short, and stocky with a reddish complexion. He has been called the toughest prosecutor in the Texas Hill Country.

A native of Junction, Sutton was graduated from Baylor University with a degree in business and was admitted to the bar following completion of law school at St. Mary's in San Antonio.

In September 1977, he was appointed by Texas Governor Dolph Briscoe as District Attorney of the 198th District in his home town and has won reelection ever since.

His main claim to fame was the tenacious — some call it obsessive — pursuit and prosecution of convicted baby killer, Nurse Genene Jones. That tale was outlined in a book entitled *Deadly Medicine*.

Sutton was raised in the Texas Hill Country, the son of Leonard Sutton, brother of Leita Nobles. Leonard Sutton was the one Olgie Nobles worked for until he opened his own business in San Angelo.

When Sutton learned that someone had tried to poison his aunt, he started his own investigation, although San Angelo (Tom Green County) was not under his jurisdiction.

Until he learned of the poisoning of Leita, Sutton had no

reason to think his uncle's death a few months earlier was due to anything but natural causes. He knew that Olgie smoked all his life and was a heavy drinker. But because he learned that his symptoms were the same as Leita's, he knew immediately that his uncle had been murdered.

He convinced the two men in charge of the investigation, Tom Green Sheriff's Investigator Bill McCloud and San Angelo based Texas Ranger George Frasier, that they had a case of murder and attempted murder on their hands. Once that was decided, there was never any suspect other than Tim Scoggin.

Sutton prepared the necessary paperwork to have his uncle's body exhumed for evidence of poison. Then he helped subpoena Scoggin's financial records. During conversations with his aunt, Sutton learned of the friendship of Scoggin and the Norton sisters and their deaths only a few months earlier.

He passed this information along to Frasier who telephoned his colleague, Texas Ranger John Waldrip in Llano.

This was the first inkling that the deaths of the Norton sisters had been anything but natural. Their death certificates read that the deaths were due to natural causes.

After all, both were known to be elderly and not in the best of health, although Catherine (Girlie) Norton had just undergone a physical at Scott & White Clinic in Temple, Texas. This conversation between the two Rangers was the first link between Olgie Nobles' death and the death of the sisters.

When Frasier called Waldrip, the Llano Ranger remembered Scoggin from the 1983 investigation of the missing contents of a safe in the Norton home. Waldrip knew it had to be an inside job as there were no signs of a forced entry. Cordelia Norton had called a halt to the investigation when lawmen wanted to question her friends. She didn't want them to be insulted.

Sutton arranged a meeting for August 24, 1988, of all investigators of the two counties on the case. That included himself, McCloud, the two Texas Rangers, Llano County District Attorney Sam Oatman and Tom Green County Assistant DA Steve Smith, heir apparent to the DA's job as his boss (Dick Alcala) was a candidate for district judge.

In that meeting, the lawmen went over Scoggin's financial records. They found an interesting link to the missing contents of the Norton safe including a declaration of sale of $650,000 in stocks, a declaration listed on his income tax, and the listing of fifty Krugerrands among his assets.

The subsequent investigation showed that Scoggin, about the time of the theft of the safe's contents, rented a safe deposit box at a San Angelo bank on August 30, 1983. He last entered the box on September 26, 1983. Dallas coin dealers purchased thirty-five Kruggerands from Scoggin at $412 each on September 19, 1983.

During that meeting, in a telephone call, Sutton talked with the San Antonio Medical Examiner's office about the tests on the exhumed body of his uncle. The results nailed the investigation when he was told Olgie Nobles died of acute arsenic poisoning.

That prompted Oatman to proceed with having the ashes of the Norton sisters exhumed for examination. Evidence of arsenic cannot be destroyed, even by cremation. Cordelia was killed by arsenic but Girlie's remains showed no evidence of arsenic. The thought was that she was poisoned by strychnine which leaves few traces and none that can be detected in ashes. Strychnine works faster than arsenic which could explain why she died soon after returning from a physical exam, getting a clean bill of health.

Strychnine is not a heavy metal so it is difficult to trace although it is odorless and tasteless and can also be administered in food and drink. Unlike arsenic, a small dosage is fatal within just a few hours.

All investigators proceeded to look more closely at the Nobles and Norton homes for evidence on how the victims were poisoned.

Lawmen had already searched the Nobles home once but went back again after talking to Mrs. Nobles and finding out she had been living on 7-Up and Riopan-Plus. Samples were taken of everything. An empty bottle of Riopan-Plus found in a trash can in Leita's bedroom had what tested to be traces of arsenic.

Arsenic is a white powder normally used to kill rats and

pests. It has no odor or taste and can be administered in food or liquid. Symptoms of arsenic poisoning may not become evident until several hours before death.

In an August 25, 1988, search of the suspect's San Angelo home by deputies, Constable Robert Holberg and Texas Ranger Frasier, several containers of white powder were found.

Evidence in the case was falling into place. Now it would be up to the district attorney's office to see if they could put together charges that would stand up in court.

CHAPTER IX

Nearing the End

Tim Scoggin's fall from grace came quickly.

After Leita Nobles' admission to Shannon Memorial Center in San Angelo, Tim continued to be as attentive as ever. He brought the mail and did whatever errands she needed done as well as look out after her son, Butch.

He was also busy in another way as he had obtained counter checks at Citizens' State Bank in Miles, a small community near San Angelo where the Nobles did their banking business.

Scoggin made sure that Leita didn't get her bank statements. From May 12 to July 28, he deposited nine checks drawn on Leita's account totaling more than $38,000 into his account at a San Angelo bank. The checks bore Leita's name for a signature even though she was in the hospital paralyzed.

Bank officials finally got curious about the signatures and then found out Leita was in the hospital where they contacted her and determined for sure the signatures were forgeries.

The checks ranged in amounts from $1,000 to $15,000. Leita confronted Scoggin about the checks. He admitted doing it, saying he needed the money. He pleaded for her help to get him out of the mess. He also asked the bank to let him pay the money back.

Shortly after Scoggin realized he was in trouble, a friend of his disappeared for two weeks, a disappearance that led to speculation that the money Scoggin had acquired by whatever means had made its way to a Swiss bank account. There was never any confirmation to this speculation.

A complaint was filed with Justice of the Peace Ruth Nicholson. Scoggin was arrested August 16, 1988, and charged with aggravated theft over $20,000, a second-degree felony. He was released the next day on $20,000 bond. Scoggin was represented by San Angelo attorneys Dan Edwards and Steve Lupton.

On August 30, 1988, Scoggin filed Chapter 7 bankruptcy in the San Angelo bankruptcy court. The bankruptcy petition showed he had twenty-two creditors. The amount of priority debts was $1,582.87; amount of secured debts was $362,000; the total of unsecured debts was $88,708.48 and total value of assets was $307,072.05.

All during this time, there was an investigation going on regarding a suspicious signature on the account of Catherine Norton for $30,000 at Fredericksburg, Texas. That check, it was discovered, was deposited in Scoggin's account at a San Angelo bank. It had been written the day before she died in February 1988 and deposited several days after she died.

On September 6, 1988, Scoggin was charged in Llano with theft by check on the Norton case with bond being set at $500,000. District Attorney Sam Oatman in Llano said the high bond was justified because he was told Scoggin might be in flight.

He was arrested that night shortly before midnight at the Midland home of his parents. That was his last taste of freedom.

Scoggin's lawyers requested that the bond be lowered. He and his father supplied evidence in a bond reduction hearing held in Burnet, a neighboring community of Llano, the next week that Scoggin left his San Angelo apartment because his business was bankrupt and he could not afford rent. He had moved in with his parents and planned to live there.

However, Oatman argued that Scoggin left the San Angelo apartment without leaving a forwarding address. District Court Judge Bob Wright reduced the bond to $35,000, and ordered Scoggin to report daily to an adult probation officer while living at the Midland home of his parents.

However, Scoggin was unable to raise that bail money and had to ask the court to appoint him an attorney for defense against the Llano charges. Money for defense on the San Angelo charges was paid by Scoggin's parents, reportedly in the range of $30,000.

A Tom Green County grand jury handed down indictments against Scoggin on October 7, 1988, for the poisoning murder of Olgie Noble, the attempted poisoning murder of Leita Noble and felony theft.

The Llano County grand jury on October 27, 1988, indicted Scoggin on two counts of murder in the deaths of Cordelia and Catherine Norton and felony theft by forgery. Bond on each murder indictment was $75,000 and $35,000 was the bond for the felony theft.

Scoggin's attorneys, Lupton & Edwards, maintained that their client was innocent of all charges and would enter not-guilty pleas.

Following arraignment on charges, the legal wrangling began. Pre-trial hearings were held. Several court dates were postponed. Prosecutors in the case appeared to be stalling in the hope the other county would take the case to court first.

It was obvious from the outset that this would be an expensive case to prosecute because of all the witnesses and expert testimony that would be needed. It was also not known if evidence from all the cases would be admissible in one trial. Llano County is relatively poor and Oatman hoped that San Angelo would go first. At the same time, San Angelo had a busy case load and there was a change in the district attorney's office with Dick Alcala having been elected to a judgeship and Stephen Smith, Alcala's assistant, elected to replace him.

All evidence in the case was circumstantial. The prosecution had evidence that Scoggin had access to strychnine and arsenic and he had access to the victims by which to administer the poison.

But there was no proof that Catherine Norton was actually killed. There were only suspicions because of her quick death just one day before the death of her sister, Cordelia.

The wheels of justice begin their slow grind with Scoggin arraigned in District Court in Llano on November 7, 1988, before Judge D. V. Hammond. Scoggin sat quietly in district court on the second floor of the Llano County courthouse.

Several civil cases were heard with District Attorney Sam Oatman scurrying in and out of the courtroom as he worked with a newly enpaneled grand jury and prepared for several arraignments. Scoggin, as always, was dapperly dressed with his gold frame glasses, not a hair out of place, his mustache combed and trimmed, wearing a pink pullover shirt and blue jeans. He looked about the courtroom without apparent nervousness, noting any attention that was drawn to him by spectators.

When he was called to the Judge's bench, Scoggin, in his very quiet voice, requested a court appointed attorney. Judge Hammond asked about his attorney of record, Steve Lupton. Scoggin said he had talked with his attorney the past week and learned about his legal costs in the San Angelo case, saying that would take all the money he had. He told the judge he had filed for bankruptcy.

When asked about his assets and liabilities, he was unable to answer except to say he did own an apartment complex. When Oatman was appraised of the situation, he requested that the arraignment be passed until the necessary paperwork could be obtained from the bankruptcy attorney, G. H. Lampley, in San Angelo.

Scoggin spoke in quiet, polite terms throughout the hearing. After his case was passed and that of another prisoner was heard, the judge directed that Scoggin and the other prisoner be taken back to jail. Outside the courtroom, both prisoners were handcuffed together and escorted through the early morning sun of this autumn day to the Llano County Jail across the street from the courthouse.

When Scoggin was escorted back to the courthouse it was the afternoon of December 5, 1988. The day was partly cloudy with temperatures in the low sixties and a slight wind made it chilly. Scoggin was escorted by a deputy and Sheriff Gale Ligon. When he noticed photographers waiting, he ducked behind one of two other prisoners being escorted along with him.

In court, Scoggin sat unsmiling, looking drawn and tense. He was wearing a maroon sweater over a plaid sports shirt and blue jeans with his usual brown loafers. He sat on the front bench of the courtroom.

Judge D. V. Hammond was again presiding and called cases 4219, 4220, and 4221. The Judge appointed Eddie Shell, the public defender for neighboring Burnet County and Shell's partner, Paul DeCuir, Jr., to defend Scoggin. The two attorneys were appointed to represent a number of defendants arraigned that afternoon.

After the appointment, Judge Hammond asked DeCuir (Shell was not present) if he wanted to confer with his client about the arraignment. He said he did and both he and Scoggin went to the back of the courtroom. The two made quite a contrast as Scoggin was a very small man. On the other hand, DeCuir, while short, is very large with a full beard and balding head. He wore a gray and black, tweed sport coat.

Following the conference, DeCuir announced that Scoggin would waive arraignment, meaning that he was aware of the charges and did not have to have them read to him and that he pleaded not guilty in writing and signed the waiver sheet. Scoggin did not make any public statements during the arraignment. Following the arraignment, he was escorted back across the street to jail.

Scoggin spent that Christmas in Llano's jail. Shortly afterwards, he was transferred to San Angelo where he conferred with his attorneys there, Steve Lupton and Dan Edwards, as they prepared for a San Angelo pre-trial hearing on January 3, 1989.

On that morning, the defense attorneys filed a motion requesting a change of venue, a request to have the trial held in some other city, citing publicity would not make it possible for Scoggin to get a fair trial in San Angelo.

During the hearing that afternoon, District Judge John Sutton — no kin to Leita Nobles or Ron Sutton — said he would take the case under advisement and make a ruling on January 24. The Judge instructed the court clerk to keep open a one- and one-half hour block for the hearing on that date. Edwards also asked at that time that a defense expert be able to examine a bottle of antacid and strands of hair that the prosecution had tested.

During the hearing, the judge noted that he might change the location of the trial to Del Rio or Fort Stockton, both not far distant. Edwards protested the consideration of Del Rio and Fort Stockton because both are in the circulation area of the San Angelo *Standard-Times*, a daily newspaper that is well circulated in West Texas.

However, Sutton was not buying the protest as he cited a case he had moved from San Angelo to Ballinger, a small town not fifty miles from San Angelo, where no one had heard of the case in question and Ballinger was far closer to San Angelo than either Del Rio or Fort Stockton.

There was some discussion over when the defense and prosecution would be ready to go to trial, and while the defense said they would be ready by March 1, District Attorney Stephen Smith said he wouldn't be until after April 1, possibly earlier. Smith said he had other cases coming up that would complicate his schedule.

On that appointed day for the change of venue hearing, Scoggin was escorted by sheriff's deputies across the street from the Tom Green County Jail to the Tom Green County Courthouse. Scoggin as always was well groomed, this time wearing jail greens and the usual brown penny loafers. He was represented by Edwards and Lupton and the state by 119th District Attorney Smith and 51st District Attorney Gerald Fohn.

After initial sparring between defense and prosecuting attorneys over the request for change of venue, both sides named witnesses to be called. All were to stay outside the courtroom so they could not hear what others had to say. The exception to that was San Angelo *Standard-Times* reporter Jeff Lison who was called on first to testify so that he could cover the rest of the hearing for his newspaper.

He said he had reported on the courts and county government for about two years. He noted that his newspaper covered fifty to fifty-four counties in circulation. He said he didn't know the extent of circulation in those counties but that the total circulation of the *Standard-Times* was about 40,000.

He viewed copies of articles he had written and verified that they appeared to be authentic and then the articles were entered into evidence.

Edwards and Lupton then called Theodore Hargrove III, a private attorney in San Angelo, to the stand. Hargrove is the defense attorney on a number of criminal cases in Tom Green County. He testified that he was familiar with the case because of newspaper articles and said he didn't believe Scoggin could get a fair trial in San Angelo. He noted that Scoggin being an undertaker would make people think of the case as being macabre and that would make it difficult to get an impartial jury.

He later testified under questioning from the state that there could probably be twelve people in the county who had not heard of the case.

Next witness for the defense was Jimmy D. Lummus, a podiatrist, who has been in practice in San Angelo since 1985. He said he sees about 100 people per week. Active in church and social work, he testified that he had talked to a number of people about the case. About twice as many knew about the case as didn't know (a ratio of 100 to 200).

The defense then called Terry Sevart, owner of a children's shoe store, to the stand and he was asked about how many people he saw per week. He said about 400 to 500 came in his store each week and had heard talk about the case. They didn't have much to say about it. The prosecution quizzed each witness about where people lived who were talking about the case — Wall, Christoval, Carlsbad, Grape Creek and other small communities around San Angelo.

David Peters, assistant vice-president of Texas Bank for seven years, said he had heard of the case through the newspaper and had heard people talking about it at the bank.

Sheriff Ernest Haynes, a thirty-year veteran of law enforcement, said he had heard people talking about the case but a lot of them didn't know anything about it. He thought there was little news exposure on the case. When asked if he was against moving the trial, he said yes as it would cost the taxpayers money. When asked by the defense if moving the trial would cause a hardship on his office, he replied, "Not particularly."

47

Judge Sutton was obviously not impressed and quickly ruled that the news coverage was not inflammatory and not excessive and denied the change of venue request.

The defense objected to the ruling. The judge noted that during the effort to seat a jury, should it be evident that a fair and impartial panel could not be seated, then he would again entertain a motion for change of venue.

A trial date was set for April 17, 1989 in Tom Green County. Llano County was holding off to see what would happen in the San Angelo cases.

The normal standard in Tom Green County is to have pre-trial hearings on all cases coming up on the first Tuesday of each month. Scoggin's cases were in that group to be heard on March 7, 1989. The usual cast of characters was there with Judge Sutton presiding, District Attorney Smith and defense attorneys Edwards & Lupton.

Scoggin was very animated during this session as he chatted with two older women seated behind him. He told them about taking a test in a correspondence course he was taking. He later exchanged glances with a dark haired woman about his age who came in and stayed for a short time and then left. Scoggin appeared to be getting accustomed to confinement as he looked less drawn and more relaxed.

Judge Sutton was adamant about meeting the trial date of April 17. He constantly told attorneys that everything should be taken care of regarding the defense discovery motions for evidence held by the prosecution well in advance so there would be no surprises.

The first part of the hearing involved whispers at the bench and a conference with the judge in chambers. All that turned out to be was legal mumbo-jumbo regarding logistics of jury selection.

The judge went over sixteen items, one by one, on the defense motion for discovery, granted almost all but one that did not apply which referred to co-defendants. He also did not act on several items that had already been taken care of. A number of these motions required conversation, with the judge finding humor in the need for several of them including introducing a previous record of the defendant which there is none. But the defense wanted it in case there was someone with the same name and it got introduced in error. The prosecution agreed that wouldn't be done. Smith seemed disgusted at times over the way it appeared that the defense attorneys were making him out to be stupid. He didn't like the fact that the defense doubted his intelligence by saying he might introduce some items that would obviously result in a mistrial.

There was a request by the defense for the names of all witnesses as well as the criminal records of all witnesses. This also caused some heated debate. It appeared the defense was using some kind of standard form for discovery motions with some items not even remotely related to the Scoggin case.

Edwards requested at least 10cc's of contents of a bottle of antacid and samples of strands of hair taken from Mrs. Nobles. This also caused much discussion along with other motions on the state's need to maintain custody of evidence. If enough was available, it was finally agreed that the state's experts would send whatever was wanted to the defense to examine. The judge expressed concern that the defense have enough time to have all items examined as well as to talk to all potential witnesses for the state.

Edwards also said he needed two to three grams of ashes of each of the cremated remains of the Norton sisters to examine. "We can't get it from Llano," Edwards said. There were other indications that Llano was not cooperating with the defense. Edwards said all this evidence was needed in the event the Llano charges were admitted during the San Angelo trial.

Smith said he intended to go to Llano later in the week to talk with Sam Oatman. The judge instructed that if what was needed was not forthcoming, to let him know and he'd issue a court order for it. That included the Norton autopsy reports. The judge set March 24 as the deadline for receiving information from Llano and March 31 as the deadline for the prosecution to have a complete list of witnesses to the defense. Smith countered with the argument that the defense had access to all files which contained names of all potential witnesses as well as all other information.

Another pre-trial was set for the following month on April 4. However, both sides were prepared for the trial. Scoggin would soon find out his fate.

CHAPTER X

The Cast of Characters

A courtroom is not the place where you expect to find humor, especially when there is a murder trial going on.

The court of Judge John Ewing Sutton is a bit different. He's not the big silent type, but rather smaller than average. He likes to talk. He's always drinking Coca-Cola from a University of Texas mug. Apparently he had trouble talking when he was a youngster and had to take speech therapy. He hasn't stopped talking since.

He comes to the bench with a lot of judicial history behind him. His grandfather was a judge in a neighboring district, but located in the same courthouse for some fifty years. He also had an uncle who was a judge. His father was a law professor at the University of Texas at Austin and his mother retired from the opinions division of the Texas attorney general's office.

UT is where the younger Sutton was educated, graduating with an accounting degree in 1973, a law degree in 1976 and passed his certified public accountant exam in 1976. He at first worked in the tax division for a major accounting firm, taking on such accounts as that of the famed H. L. Hunt. He returned to his home town of San Angelo in 1977 to join a firm founded in 1904. He became a partner in 1981 in that firm, Shannon, Porter, Johnson and Sutton.

In May 1987, Sutton was appointed judge of the 119th district by Texas Governor Bill Clements. He didn't take the bench immediately as he was involved in a case.

This was a major career move for him as previously he had been involved in federal laws, mostly concerning taxes. Now he is involved with state law. It also meant a major change in his flamboyant life style as a judge's pay is not anywhere near what he was making in private practice.

His hobbies required considerable income, such as being a pilot with commercial and instrument ratings and a licensed flight instructor, being a scuba diver and travelling all over to dip into clear waters.

He is married and the father of two children.

Sutton's court is something like that on the popular television show of the late 1980's and early 1990's, *Night Court*. His temporary bailiff, who volunteered to be bailiff for the Scoggin trial, is somewhat similar to Bull Shannon on the television show. Joe Stapp is a big man with a sense of humor but the resemblance to Bull Shannon ends there.

Stapp was born in Fredericksburg, Texas, in 1953, grew up in the small West Texas town of Monahans and entered police work in that county with the city of Monahans and then moved on to work for the county in which it is in, becoming chief deputy sheriff. In 1983, he joined the Tom Green County sheriff's office, does patrol work and some court work.

The sheriff's officer assigned to escort Tim Scoggin from the jail to the courthouse was Ray Davis, who was born in 1944 in Tahoka, Texas, but lived most of his life in San Angelo. He is a third generation lawman and started with the Tom Green County Sheriff's office as a reserve in 1974, going full time in 1980.

On the defense team for Scoggin was Dan Edwards, Steve Lupton and their legal assistant Jolena Hawkins Mida. All are native West Texans.

Daniel A. Edwards was born April 9, 1951 in Big Lake, Texas, a small community near San Angelo, the son of a lawyer. He was graduated from Angelo State University in San Angelo with a BA in English/Interpersonal Communication, received a certificate in secondary education from Texas Tech

University graduate school and graduated from Texas Tech University Law School in December 1982.

Before going to college, he was in the United States Air Force and later the Texas Air National Guard. After receiving his teacher's certificate, he taught school at his hometown and at Midland College campus in his hometown. Following law school, he practiced law with his father, Aubrey Edwards in Big Lake, then joined the district attorney's office in San Angelo (Tom Green County). Edwards entered private practice again in 1986 and formed a partnership with Lupton August 18, 1988.

Stephen R. Lupton, born November 13, 1955 in San Angelo, graduated from the University of Texas at Austin in 1978 with a BA in government and then went on to Texas Tech University Law school from where he was graduated in 1981. He joined the Harris County (Houston) district attorney's office where he worked for two years before moving back to his hometown and joining the law firm of Davis, Wardlaw, Hay & Wittenburg. After two years, he started his own practice in 1985 and later that year he joined the staff of the Tom Green County District Attorney's office where he met Edwards.

Lupton went back into private practice in 1987 and formed the partnership with Edwards in 1988.

Mida, born October 30, 1953, in San Angelo, is the wife of a San Angelo policeman, Steven Alan Mida. She has worked as a secretary since graduating from Central High School in San Angelo in 1972. Mida also attended Angelo State University. She became a legal secretary in 1977 and received national certification as a professional legal secretary in March 1988. She joined Edwards & Lupton as a legal assistant on September 1, 1988.

On the other side of the room were representatives of the state. Ron Sutton was there but only in an unofficial capacity. District Attorney Stephen Smith was in charge of the prosecution. The burden of proving guilt was on his shoulders.

Not only was this a difficult case, but it was one of Smith's first as DA. He was sworn into that position only a few months earlier on January 1, 1989. Born March 7, 1954, in Laurel, Mississippi, Smith attended Baylor University and Law School in Waco, Texas, then served almost five years in the Air Force before looking for a job.

One of his interviews was in the county attorney's office in Tom Green (San Angelo) County. He and his wife liked the looks of the town so he accepted the job. A year later, in February 1986, he joined the district attorney's office and then sought election to that position when his boss, Dick Alcala, ran for district judge.

Going into the trial, Smith had no doubt of Scoggin's guilt. But knowing it and proving it in court are two different things. The outcome would depend on what he was allowed to introduce in court as evidence and testimony and to be able to destroy evidence by the defense team.

Also at the prosecutor's table was Assistant District Attorney Charlotte Harris. Born January 14, 1951, in Amarillo, Texas, she attended Henderson County Junior College, Texas Tech University in Lubbock, Texas, and earned her degree from the University of Texas at Austin. She then went on to law school at the University of Houston where she graduated in 1978. While working at the law school after graduation, she also had a private practice and then moved on to nearby Columbus. After that she went to Wichita Falls where she became the first public defender in that city.

In 1988, she joined the Tom Green County DA's office. For her, the Scoggin case was a challenge. She knew he was guilty but getting that over to a jury through evidence and evidence the court would deem to be admissible was the question at hand.

On the morning of April 17, 1989, this group gathered along with a crowd of about 150 Tom Green County residents and numerous spectators in the spacious second floor courtroom of the County Courthouse. It was the monthly court call for that court and three others. The 150 potential jurors obviously were from all walks of life and were attired in various fashions from suits and ties for men to fashionable dresses for the ladies down to and including what one might wear to the beach.

The defense and prosecutors were in uniform of conserv-

53

ative attire with dark clothes and the three men wore red ties. Scoggin wore a brown suit with a mild, plaid pattern, a brown tie, white shirt and the usual penny loafers he always wore.

It was a nice, typical spring day for West Texas, with the sun breaking out and warming what had been a slightly chilly night. The temperatures warmed up the area to a point where the jury panel was complaining about the courtroom being hot.

Judge Sutton proved to be an ice breaker and spoke of his fondness for talking, even though he had speech therapy for four years in elementary school. He used any time available for a civics lesson on the Texas justice system. He noted it is not like what potential jurors may have seen on television. He said that the defense and state each have ten pre-emptive choices from the jury panel and there would be jurors excused for cause.

Of those selected, the panel was cut to eighty and the Judge likened it to winning the lottery. When the list of eighty came back from the clerk's office, Scoggin went through it and made marks beside several names to advise his attorneys of potential problems.

After lunch, Judge Sutton read charges to the jury panel — theft from the Nobles between May 18 and July 28, 1988; attempted murder of Leita Nobles between December 12, 1987 and May 27, 1988; and murder of Olgie Nobles on or about March 23, 1988.

The theft is a second degree felony carrying a penalty of two to twenty years and a fine not to exceed $10,000; the attempted murder was a second degree felony carrying a penalty of two to twenty years and/or a fine not to exceed $10,000 and murder, a first degree felony carrying a penalty of from five years to ninety-nine or life and a fine not to exceed $10,000.

It was mentioned numerous times that Scoggin had applied for probated sentences should he be found guilty, as required by Texas law, and this should not be held against him. It was also repeated a number of times that it is the prerogative of the defendant whether or not to testify and, if he chose not to do so, it should not be held against him. A number of potential jurors had problems with saying they would give a probated sentence for murder.

54

A number of potential jurors were called into the judge's chambers for consultation with attorneys about what they knew about the case, when they indicated they had knowledge of the case and possibly could not be fair. The judge noted repeatedly that what some jurors thought they might know could be in error and he didn't want them talking about what their "knowledge" was in open court.

When it came time for the state to address the jury panel, Smith said the suspect should be considered innocent until proven guilty. To prove this is a burden of the state. He noted that the state had to prove beyond a reasonable doubt and not beyond any doubt or not beyond a shadow of a doubt. No one indicated among the potential jurors they had a problem with what he said.

He also explained the difference between direct evidence and circumstantial evidence. Although Texas has the death penalty, the lack of direct evidence dictated that the death penalty could not be sought against Scoggin. The jury panel did not seem to have a problem making a conviction based on circumstantial evidence. It was explained that there are two phases in a trial, determining innocence or guilt and then if guilty, the penalty phase.

Defense Attorney Dan Edwards then took over and proceeded to ask questions. On all questions, the jury panel was polled. Edwards read an extensive list of potential witnesses to see if any of the jury panel had any trouble accepting their testimony. On that list was Scoggin's parents and an aunt, all of whom were present for the jury selection.

Edwards noted that it was up to the jury to determine what weight to give testimony of each witness and also to provide their own definition of beyond a reasonable doubt. Edwards also asked if any people on the panel were kin to law enforcement people. One woman said her husband was a policeman. Edwards asked her if she could find Scoggin innocent and then go home and face her husband. She replied that she had some doubt about it.

Edwards also asked the jury panel if they had been on juries before and if the jury reached a verdict. Then he asked if any of them had been victims of crime before. There were surprisingly few victims of crime on the panel.

At one point, Edwards was dissatisfied with the possibility of some people in the first twenty or so that might get on the jury. He asked that the panel be reshuffled. Names were redrawn and called out in a different order. Edwards still wasn't pleased with the possibility of what he had to deal with.

Finally, by 6:45 P.M. that first day, a twelve-member jury had been selected. It consisted of six men and six women, which included a black woman, two Hispanic women and one Hispanic man. Most appeared to be in their late thirties and up except for one Hispanic woman who was slightly younger, about thirty.

It was a jury the state liked because of their education and ability to grasp the technicalities of the case. The defense wanted a less sophisticated group to determine their client's fate.

STONE FENCE WITH IRON GATE — *The entryway to the Norton Mansion was difficult to see from Texas Highway 29.*
— Courtesy Norton Estate, Attorney Mary Moursand, executress

THE NORTON MANSION — *It's located high on a hill just east of Llano, Texas.*
— Courtesy Norton Estate, Attorney Mary Moursand, executress

LAVISH ENTRYWAY — *The entry hall, like the rest of the mansion, was full of antiques.*

— Courtesy Norton Estate, Attorney Mary Moursand, executress

SPACIOUS ROOMS — *The Norton Mansion was large with plenty of space for oversized antique furniture collected by the Nortons from all over the world. There were many elephant figurines out of all types of materials located throughout the house, all with upturned trunks to signify good luck. One can be seen in this picture at the head of the bed.*

— Courtesy Norton Estate, Attorney Mary Moursand, executress

NORTON PRIDE — *The Nortons took great pride in their businesses and success. Norton's Flower & Dress Shop was a venture of Catherine Norton while Cordelia Norton operated the Lone Star beer distributorship in Llano.*

LLANO CEMETERY — *The Norton family burial plot is kept in immaculate shape complete with a sprinkler system. The Llano Cemetery was one of the prime beneficiaries of the Norton sisters' will.*

CLOSED BY BANKRUPTCY — *In San Angelo, Texas, Tim Scoggin's bankruptcy left Nobles Air Conditioning business closed along with his next door business, Annie Mae's Christmas & More store that he started after purchasing the air conditioning business from Olgie Nobles. The businesses were located along the scenic Rio Concho River that runs through San Angelo.*

INVESTIGATION — In October 1988, the indictment of Tim Scoggin in the deaths of Cordelia and Catherine Norton was announced in Llano during a press conference. Involved in the investigation were, left to right, Texas Ranger John Waldrip, Llano County Sheriff Gale Ligon, District Attorney Sam Oatman and DA Investigator Henry Nolan.

UNDER ARREST — Tim Scoggin arrested in Midland, Texas, on August 16, 1988, initially for aggravated theft over $20,000. He was later charged and indicted in the deaths of Cordelia Norton, Catherine Norton, and Olgie Nobles and the attempted murder of Leita Nobles with the use of a deadly weapon — poison. He is pictured being escorted to a pre-trial hearing in San Angelo.

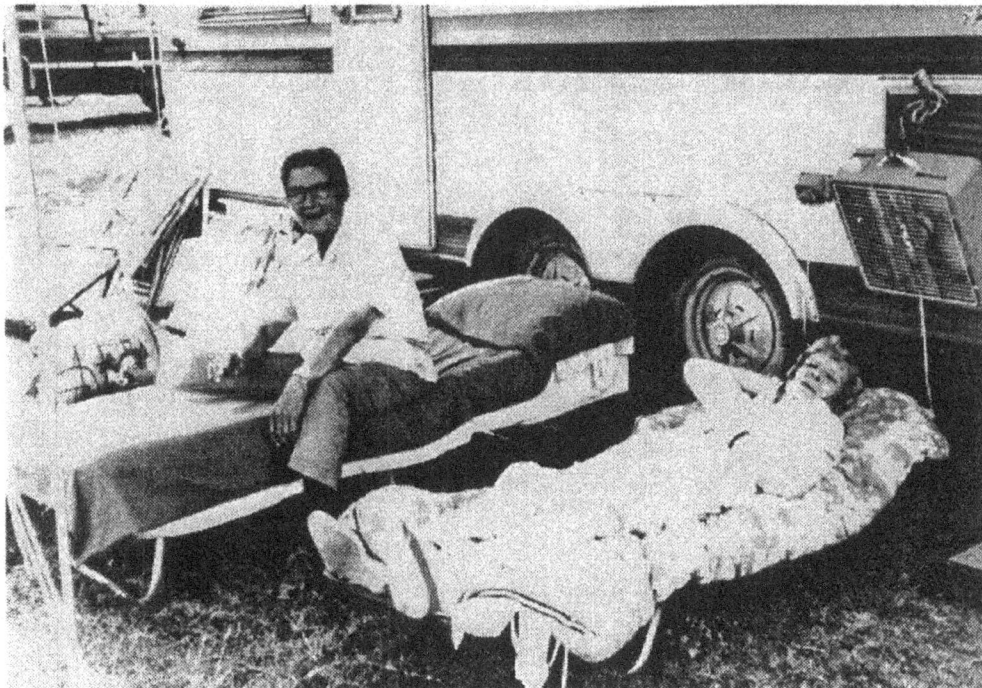

VICTIMS 1 & 2 — Cordelia Norton, left, and Catherine (Girlie) Norton, pictured on one of their many outdoor excursions, died within one day of each other in February 1988.

— Courtesy of Norton Family Friend,
T. D. Swenson

VICTIM 3 — Olgie Nobles died in March 1988. His body was later exhumed for an examination that showed he died of arsenic poisoning. A camera shy Nobles is pictured in one of few pictures that exist of him.

INTENDED VICTIM — Leita Nobles is still recovering from an attempt on her life with arsenic. She has made a miraculous recovery.

CHAPTER XI

Trial — Day 1

The trial of Tim Scoggin promised to be full of surprises as the prosecution was saddled with trying to prove he poisoned Olgie and Leita Nobles and the defense trying to paint a picture of innocence.

The first surprise came quickly. After having previously entered pleas of not guilty to all charges, Scoggin on the first day of his trial following the day of jury selection, entered a plea of guilty to the charge of theft on writing checks on the Nobles' account. The change of plea came before the jury was brought in. Judge Sutton told Scoggin of his rights.

When the jury came in, they were told of Scoggin's change of plea. This appeared to be a clever strategy on the part of the defense as they knew the prosecution had a strong case against Scoggin on the check writing theft. They also knew that the state didn't have a strong, locked up case on the murder and attempted murder cases. It was evident they wanted to keep the jury from thinking that if he pled innocent to all charges, that if one case was proven, he might be guilty on all charges.

It was also apparent that the defense might want the jury to believe Scoggin was just trying to salvage a failing business so that he could get the Nobles paid what was owed them. He was trying to do them a favor and planned to eventually repay what he had stolen from them.

Assistant DA Charlotte Harris made the opening statement for the state, saying the prosecution intends to prove that Scoggin had woven a web of deceit and greed to take advantage of those who trusted him. She recapped the relationship of the Nobles and Scoggin and events leading up to Olgie's death and Leita's hospitalization. Harris also noted that while the two had gruff personalities and called each other the old lady and old man, they still had a strong bond, having been married since 1942.

Harris said the state will present motive.

Defense Attorney Dan Edwards made the opening statement for the defense. True, Tim made a bad mistake, Edwards started out, but he added that he is willing to pay for this mistake. The theft is why the finger has been pointed at him for the arsenic poisoning, Edwards added, then he compared the investigation to a road map but lawmen had on blinders. They missed many exits, according to Edwards' beliefs.

Carol Gene Gober, an attractive woman, was the first witness for the prosecution. A woman of about forty, she was a neighbor of the Nobles and had sold them their place in Grape Creek northwest of San Angelo. She had known them about six years and was closest to Mr. Nobles. The Nobles considered her kids their grandchildren. They were good neighbors, Gober related. She had a key to their house to look after Mr. Nobles when Mrs. Nobles went back to work after Olgie's accident.

She was the one who reported the suspected arsenic poisoning to the sheriff's office after she had made a visit to Mrs. Nobles hospital room and talked to her and doctors. Mrs. Nobles told her what to tell the sheriff's office and what to look for in the house, an open 7-Up bottle in the refrigerator and a brown jar on the back porch with white powder in it. That was the only powder Mrs. Nobles knew of in the house.

Gober had known Scoggin since he bought the Nobles' business. She had not gone to see Mrs. Nobles right away after Olgie died as she thought Leita might just be sick from nerves and needed to rest for a while. Gober had seen Scoggin's Lincoln at the house a number of times before Olgie died, but not afterwards.

Defense Attorney Steve Lupton questioned Gober for the defense and made a number of attempts to paint a sordid picture. He implied there was something funny going on between her and Mr. Nobles and that Mrs. Nobles knew about it and was mad. After all, Olgie had an eye for the ladies. He also implied that Mrs. Nobles was upset over a gift he had given Mrs. Gober.

"Not so," Gober retorted, at least she wasn't aware of it and didn't know if Mrs. Nobles was ever upset at her. Lupton then tried to get Gober to testify about trouble between the Nobles.

Gober said she never knew two people who loved each other more than the Nobles. Lupton asked when locks were changed on the Nobles house as if to imply Mrs. Nobles didn't want Gober in the house. She said she didn't know. He also asked about $700 missing from Mrs. Nobles' billfold after the accident and before Mr. Nobles died. Two yard girls were implicated as the defense seemed to be making an effort to point accusing fingers in all directions. Lupton tried to imply there was something wrong about the relationship between Mr. Nobles and the yard girls but Gober said she didn't know about it.

Defense questions appeared to be straw grabbing efforts as Lupton attempted to cast suspicious away from his client. Mrs. Gober also told Lupton she had borrowed about $900 from Mr. Nobles for car repairs. She also noted that she had well water tested at the Nobles home for arsenic.

Second witness was Dr. Robert Lee Carsner, an internist. He has been a physician in San Angelo since 1975 and has a clinic. He had cared for Mrs. Nobles for about five years before the poisoning. He saw her five days before she was admitted to the San Angelo hospital. At that time, he diagnosed her as having a peptic ulcer. Five days later she was admitted to the hospital through the emergency room, complaining of being weak and having nausea, vomiting and abdominal pain. She had gastrointestinal bleeding, her blood count had dropped. She was given transfusions as well as fed by tubes.

Then before the eyes of people at the hospital, she became paralyzed.

Dr. Carsner called in another doctor to give tests for heavy metal poisoning. She complained of tingling in her arms and legs. She was in acute care for one month, paralyzed for three weeks and couldn't do anything for herself. She was in the hospital for four months. Dr. T. W. Carpenter gave her tests for arsenic which showed she had 300 milligrams per million with 80 being normal. He testified she is now doing better than ever thought possible and is undergoing therapy, being able to care for herself and her son.

Under questioning by the defense, Dr. Carsner said he had been treating Mrs. Nobles for five years for high blood pressure. She was on medication. He said after a large dose of arsenic, it would take five to seven days for symptoms to appear. Classic symptoms are paralyzed nerves in the extremities. It can cause blotchy skin, which Mrs. Nobles didn't have. It can cause delusions. She didn't have these until later. He had never treated arsenic poisoning before.

Dr. Carpenter, a neurologist, was called to the stand. He had only witnessed one other arsenic poisoning before and he knew that because the husband confessed to poisoning his wife. He noted that arsenic interferes with bodily functions.

Gary Deitikier, sanitarian for Tom Green County, was next. He tested water in the well at the Nobles place for possible contamination. He was questioned about the conditions of the containers used to send water samples to the lab on June 30, 1988. He testified they were clean.

William Poe testified that the well water contained far less arsenic than the state standard for being safe.

After lunch, lawmen begin taking the stand with the first being Lou Hargraves, criminal investigator for the sheriff's office, an office he had held for eight years. He testified that on June 14, 1988, he went with Mrs. Gober to the Nobles home, looking for specified containers, an open 7-Up bottle — which was not found — and a brown jar with white powder, also not found. About ten days later, investigators got the 7-Up bottle from a relative who found it in the house but the bottle didn't have anything in it. Hargraves went off the investigation after

August 1, 1988, as he was going on vacation. He didn't feel like the investigation could wait until he got back. There was not a thorough search of the Nobles home, he testified.

On cross examination, there was obvious hostility between Hargraves and Lupton as the defense attorney bore down on what could have been inferred as incompetence in the investigation.

Texas Ranger George Frasier, a veteran of the famed Texas Rangers for fourteen years and with the Texas Department of Public Safety for twenty-two years, was the next to take the stand. He was called into the investigation in July by the sheriff's office. He went with a sheriff's officer to the Nobles home on August 3 looking for antacid bottles and baby food jars. They didn't' find any baby food jars but got six bottles of antacid, four from the refrigerator and two from a table in Mrs. Nobles' bedroom.

Again, Frasier reported, there was not a thorough search of the Nobles Home. They were looking for something that was used only by the Nobles as their son had never gotten sick and neither had out-of-town guests.

A very cool, calm Ranger pointed out on a sketch of the Nobles home where the bottles were found and reported that only one bottle of Riopan-Plus had a positive testing for arsenic. He reported that he had searched the Scoggin residence September 25, 1988 and at another time the Scoggin business was checked out, but nothing seized tested positive for poison. Photos of the antacid bottles were introduced into evidence. He was asked if any other photos were taken and he said there weren't.

He later returned to the stand and recanted that testimony and mentioned a Tylenol bottle of which a picture was taken.

Defense attorneys asked about a Tylenol bottle taken by the Ranger from the kitchen sink area. Frasier said it was not tested. There was constant questioning by defense and prosecutors about the security of items procured for testing.

The defense hinted at the possibility of product tampering but that line of thought didn't go very far and was dropped.

Guy Abbott, co-owner of Abbott Supermarket in San Angelo was the next called to testify. He delivered what proved to be testimoney that is called the "smoking gun," evidence about the murder "weapon." He said he had known Tim (Scoggin) about eight years. Abbott related that he was in Scoggin's Christmas store next door to the air conditioning business on December 9, 1987, to make a purchase when Scoggin asked him about something to kill coons (racoons). Abbott recommended a liquid, Cowley's Original Rat and Mouse Poison. Two days later, Scoggin bought two to three bottles of it. However, in a statement to sheriff's officers earlier, he said Scoggin bought four to six bottles of the rat poison. A picture of the rat poison was introduced. It cost $1.69 a bottle.

The defense questioned Abbott hard about the difference in his statement to investigators compared to what he had said on the stand about the number of bottles of the poison purchased by Scoggin. Abbott stood by what he said on the stand.

Sheriff's Office Criminal Investigator William (Bill) McCloud, next said that only one other place around San Angelo sells Cowley's. He said a bottle of rat poison found by a Nobles relative was sent to Odessa Police Department for laser finger printing, a process that will pick up more than will traditional finger printing dusting procedures. However, nothing was found on the bottle. Where that bottle was found in the Nobles home would be divulged in testimony later.

He testified that information about the bottle was lost and not uncovered until a week before the trial when it was sent to the Texas Department of Public Safety laboratory in Austin for testing and found to have what the label said it contained. It had the same lot number stamped on it as sold by Abbott. The defense protested vigorously concerning the conclusions drawn by the lot numbers and the fact that it came from Abbott's and was the bottle purchased by Scoggin.

Javier Flores, forensic chemist for the DPS lab in Austin for five- and one-half years, testified one of the six Riopan-Plus bottles found at the Nobles home tested positive for arsenic poisoning.

J. Rod McCutcheon, with the DPS lab for eighteen years,

said the Riopan-Plus bottle had 200 parts per million in the solution in one test and 190 parts in another type of test known as atomic absorption test. He also tested the rat poison and reported that it had 1.3 per cent by weight volume arsenic in an eight ounce bottle, enough for eight fatal doses.

The defense hammered on witnesses regarding standards for testing.

Dr. Dennis James, Jr., research chemist at Texas A&M University at College Station, Texas, took hair samples from Mr. and Mrs. Nobles and found arsenic in both samples, 100 parts per million on Mr. Nobles and 95.8 parts in hair closest to the scalp of Mrs. Nobles.

Dr. James was the last of twelve witnesses on the first day of testimony which ended at 5:30 P.M.

CHAPTER XII

Trial — Day 2

The first day of testimony laid the groundwork for the defense and prosecution as the defense was trying to create doubt. Tim Scoggin's attorneys pointed fingers of accusation in all directions. On the other hand, the prosecution was zeroing in on Scoggin, showing he had purchased rat poison that contained arsenic and he had the opportunity to administer the poison on his many visits to the home of Olgie and Leita Nobles.

On the second day, Scoggin, dressed in the same suit he had worn the previous two days, appeared more concerned, his sallow complexion looking even more pasty than ever. As usual, his parents were in the courtroom.

The number of spectators was on the increase, primarily due to a report in that morning's San Angelo *Standard-Times* that Leita Nobles would be testifying that day.

First on the witness stand was Dr. James Garriott, chief toxicologist for the Bexar (San Antonio) County medical examiner's office. He had served since 1982 in that position. Previously, he served in a similar position for twelve years in Dallas County and for twelve years before that in the state of Connecticut.

He testified that hair grows about one centimeter per

month on the average individual. The amount of arsenic in the average human is .1 parts per million up to 1. On Mrs. Nobles, 8.5 parts were at the tips of her hair and 95.8 was closest to the scalp. On Mr. Nobles, his was 135 a distance from the scalp and 96.7 closest to the scalp. It takes time for arsenic to get to the hair, Garriott told questioning prosecutors and arsenic can cause death in less than one-half hour. Arsenic had been last administered to Mrs. Nobles one week to one-and one-half months before she was diagnosed and the hair shows she had been poisoned several times over a period of about eight months give or take two to three weeks. The amount of arsenic he found was 100 to 1,000 times normal.

On cross examination by defense attorney Dan Edwards, Garriott said that people who spray pesticides cannot get above the normal range of arsenic in their body. He noted that arsenic is a compound included in pesticides and herbicides and known to be in more than twenty products that can be purchased over the counter. Over a period of time, symptoms of arsenic poisoning can vary and be very subtle including nausea, diarrhea, weakness, loss of appetite, vomiting, pigmented skin, and anemia. It affects all organs of the body, he said.

Dr. J. B. Stephens of Brownwood, a physician since 1943, said he had been seeing Mrs. Nobles since 1966. She was critically ill when admitted to the Brownwood hospital on May 5. Mrs. Nobles had seen him two days earlier. She was dismissed from the hospital on May 19, 1988 and had improved markedly. Her symptoms included palor, abdominal pain, diarrhea, vomiting, unsteadiness, gastro-intestinal bleeding, a duodenal ulcer, urinary tract infection, weakness, herpes or shingles. She was given two units of blood transfusions of potassium and sodium, intravenous fluid and nutritional fluid. Dr. Stephens said he had never treated anyone for arsenic poisoning.

Mrs. Nobles first had gastrointestinal tests done in 1981, Dr. Stephens related, and she had monthly appointments with him including one on February 3, March 2, and April 5, 1988 as well as May 3. When she came for the May appointment, she reported she had been vomiting for the previous two weeks.

Next to take the stand was Leita Nobles' son, Leon (Butch) James, who gave his age as fifty-one. He has lived with his mother all of his life except two years in the U.S. Army. He lost both legs and his right eye due to diabetes and goes regularly to San Antonio and Big Spring Veterans' hospitals for treatments.

He testified that he helped care for Olgie after the accident in December 1987 and he does cooking and shopping with his mother. He first met Tim when Scoggin bought the Nobles' business. Tim came to the house two or three times when his mother wasn't there. When his mother worked for Tim, he'd go to the National Guard Armory in San Angelo for recreation. He said he didn't see Tim bring in food, although he did mention Tim had brought in some groceries at one time and Jell-O in another instance. Scoggin also would stop by to use the bathroom on his way to his parents' home in Midland, Butch said.

Butch James testified from a wheel chair.

After lunch, stipulated testimony was read to the jury from Nancy Royal, a corporal with Odessa Police, saying she had received the Cowley's Rat and Mouse Poison from the Tom Green Sheriff's office and put it into a test tank. This, like other testimony, dwelled on the security of all evidence.

Bill Houston, also a corporal with the Odessa Police, testified he tested the container for fingerprints and only found those belonging to the Nobles relatives who had found it and turned it into authorities.

Jo Kelly, with the City of Odessa Police Identification Division, said she found the can of Cowley's and sent it to the Department of Public Safety lab in Austin a week before trial started. She sent it on the request of the Tom Green Sheriff's office.

Dr. Thomas Jetter, a specialist in surgery of the jaws and face with a practice in San Angelo since 1978, saw Olgie Nobles the day he was injured, December 21, 1987 at Shannon Hospital emergency room. He had multiple facial fractures and life threatening injuries due to his age and general health — alcohol abuse and lung disorder due to smoking. Dr. Jetter said Nobles had been improving and was seeing the doctor monthly before his death.

After a brief recess, Mrs. Nobles took the stand in a wheel chair. The crowd in the courtroom had grown to about sixty people by this time. Mrs. Scoggin did not return to the courtroom after the recess. Emotions were running at high tide as Mrs. Nobles began to tell her story.

She told of having lived in Grape Creek since 1985 and she and Olgie purchased the home where she now lived in 1987, next door to the trailer where they had been living. She recapped the lives of her and her husband, saying how they had moved to San Angelo in 1962 from Junction and Brownwood and started the business with pecans, furs and air conditioners. She helped Olgie repair evaporative coolers — swamp boxes as they are commonly called.

They had met Tim (Scoggin) through a nephew who had a trailer house and the trailer park on Cactus Lane. She takes Tagament, Maalox, Riopan-Plus or Mylanta and has a bottle handy at all times. When Olgie had his wreck on December 21, 1987, she was at the business helping Scoggin who took her to the hospital. "I took care of him. He ate baby food and Half & Half (milk)," she mentioned, choked with emotion. The wreck had injured his throat as well as his jaws but he had gotten to where he could eat other things.

She told of selling the business to Scoggin and then later the buildings. He borrowed money from the bank for two buildings and she and her husband carried the note for the other two buildings. His payment was $1,700 a month. He wasn't always regular with payments and got behind especially in 1988 when he was having financial problems, Leita related. Scoggin borrowed money from Olgie to start the Christmas store and Olgie made several other loans to him to help run the business. He also borrowed $35,000 from Olgie to buy his trailer back. He paid back other small loans but she never saw a penny on the big loan.

Olgie was weak but getting better in March 1988, Leita said as she was asked about her husband's final days. Leita spoke in a very quiet voice with the crowd straining to hear every word. Scoggin appeared to be more pale than normal. On Wednesday or Thursday, he got terribly sick and vomited all over the place and had diarrhea, she continued. She was

74

also sick. She called the doctor and got medicine for Olgie. Tim picked it up and brought it to the house. Olgie got some better. The symptoms slowed down but then on Saturday night, he got really sick.

She went to bed late in her bedroom with Butch's bedroom between hers and Olgie's. She told Butch to listen for him. About an hour later, Butch woke her up and said Olgie was mumbling something. She went to him at 1:00 A.M. and he wanted to go to the bathroom but he couldn't make it and she tried to help him.

The bailiff brought in tissues for her as she was having obvious difficulty in continuing.

She gave him some medicine, a theragesic. About 3:00 A.M., she got up again and he was breathing real hard. Olgie was still in the middle of the bed where she had put him to keep him from falling off. About an hour later, she got up and he was dead. She called an ambulance and then called John Poss to meet her at the hospital. She drove there with Butch. She told Poss to call Tim. She said Tim had told her at one time that if anything happened, he would help make funeral arrangements. Tim was in Midland at the home of his parents when Poss called. Tim drove the eighty miles right away to help her make the arrangements and met her at Massey's Funeral Home. He helped pick out a casket and everything, Leita said as her testimony continued.

The next day, on Monday, he drove her out to the cemetery to pick out a burial plot. Relatives got there later that day and the funeral was Tuesday. Tim was very attentive all during this testimony with his jaws clamped tightly as if he was about to grind his teeth.

Leita said the relatives left on Saturday and then Sunday, Tim helped her address thank you cards. She was sick all week and she doesn't remember a lot about the time between then and in June when her diagnosis was made. She didn't remember Butch coming to see her in the Brownwood Hospital, a fact that really upset her. She said Tim took her to the Brownwood Hospital and came and got her. She slept a lot after getting out of the hospital in Brownwood.

She spoke of being able to walk some now but with help.

She still has no use of her hands, both of which were in a plastic type cast with brackets on top of them. When shown the Cowley's Rat and Mouse Poison, Leita said there hadn't been a varmint problem at the business since they stopped handling pecans in about 1982 or '83. She noted Tim had a key to her Post Office box and had access to her house keys while she was at work as she laid her purse out where he could get them. He would bring mail and help get groceries. Butch and Poss also went grocery shopping some. Butch was the beneficiary of her will and she was the beneficiary of Tim's will. Olgie didn't know about her will. She also told Tim she had been poisoned when he came to see her at the hospital, soon after she had told Carol Gober. He didn't seem concerned.

Following a recess, Defense Attorney Steve Lupton began cross examining Mrs. Nobles. He noted to her to make the jury aware that the business had been reopened by another owner and that she had been down to visit the new owners. He mentioned a list of assets that was made after Olgie died but she didn't seem to be aware of it. After introducing a diagram of the business buildings Scoggin had purchased, Lupton went over the uses for each building. He asked Leita if there were live traps used at the buildings because of varmint problems. She said Poss had put some there but didn't think he ever caught anything. She said she had trouble with a deep freeze being unplugged by animals and something had eaten her cat's food.

There is another floor beneath the main floor of the buildings with this floor being open at the rear. Lupton maintained that varmints were attracted to the area as the buildings were on the Concho River which winds its way through San Angelo.

The defense continued their contentions that the Cowley's poison was purchased by Scoggin to control rats, raccoons and other varmints in the area. Lupton contended that Scoggin wasn't at the Nobles home between the time Olgie was released from the hospital and the time he died but Mrs. Nobles quickly set him straight, noting that he brought out medicine and he stopped on his way to Midland to bring a loaf of bread on the Saturday Olgie died later that night. He had called to see if she needed anything.

When asked if there was any conflict between her and Carol Gober, Mrs. Nobles said no and she said Gober only came to see her once in the hospital and that's the time she told her about the diagnosis. She also changed the locks after that point and had changed the locks once before but didn't remember when. She had a great deal of difficulty in remembering various things such as who visited the house when and when she substituted for Tim at work in April so he could go to Dallas to a china painting show.

She also worked a half-day for him while he went to Midland in April. She tried to work for him when he went to Dallas but Poss sent her home after a half day as she was sick. Lupton tried to refresh her memory about whether or not Tim had called the following Monday and urged her to see a doctor. She said she didn't remember this but she had a standing doctor's appointment each month. When asked if the bottles of antacid she got were sealed, she said she was sure that she checked and she was the only one who used them. Leita also pointed out she was sure the bottle she kept at the business was Riopan-Plus, the same type that had the arsenic in it that was found at the house. Lupton implied that she couldn't be sure of that and Leita strongly asserted that, "Yes," she could.

Mrs. Nobles' testimony was interrupted as it was getting late in the day and there was another witness from out of town who needed to make airline connections.

Dr. Vincent DiMaio, chief medical examiner for Bexar County for the past eight years and formerly the ME in Dallas County, was due to testify the next morning at a capital murder case in San Antonio and his plane was due to leave San Angelo at 6:30 P.M. A sheriff's escort was waiting to take him to the airport. DiMaio is well known for his expert testimony in murder cases all over the United States.

He took the stand at almost 5:00 P.M. Dr. DiMaio did a complete autopsy beginning at 10:45 A.M., August 10, 1988. The body was brought by Lt. McCloud on the order of a justice of the peace. The medical examiner reported there were lethal amounts of arsenic in the four main organs of the body — the muscle, kidney, liver, and spleen. All tested in the lethal range. Nobles had suffered from acute arsenic poisoning and had been poisoned by arsenic at least once before. He had an enlarged heart, about 500 grams compared to a norm of 350 but this wasn't bad for a man of seventy-seven.

Nobles also had hardening of the arteries, Dr. DiMaio pointed out. He noted that arsenic poisoning is not easy to diagnose as it is so rare in recent times. It used to be the most popular way to kill people as it is odorless and tasteless. In acute cases, symptoms start immediately.

Due to the length of DiMaio's testimony, the rest of Mrs. Nobles testimony would have to wait until the next day.

CHAPTER XIII

Trial — Day 3

Tim Scoggin changed suits for the third day of testimony. This one was cream colored with the same tie as he had on before. Judge Sutton convened the proceedings at 8:30 A.M.

First witness was Leo "Boss" Sutton of New Mexico, a retired oil field pumper and brother of Leita Nobles. Leita had called him about Olgie's car accident. He visited Olgie on March 7 and stayed four or five hours. Boss came back the day after Olgie died and stayed six to seven days. Accompanying him were his wife, Sybil, and two sons. The rest of his family went back to New Mexico the day after the funeral. He testified that Leita took antacid almost every hour. He came back when Leita got out of the Brownwood hospital. Tim had called to let them know Leita was in the Brownwood Hospital. After the Brownwood stay, she complained about her hands and feet bothering her.

An ambulance was called to take her to Shannon Hospital. Contradicting other testimony, Boss said Tim suggested calling an ambulance and made the call. He said Leita had wanted to go by ambulance to the Brownwood hospital in early May but the San Angelo ambulance service couldn't go that far out of town as the service doesn't have enough spare equipment to have a unit gone for an extended period.

Under cross examination, Boss told Lupton that after Leita found out she had been poisoned, she wanted locks on her home changed and he changed them.

Sybil Sutton, wife of Boss for almost fifty years, was next on the witness stand. Leita was sick, she said, after Olgie's death. She drank a lot of milk and took a lot of antacids. Leita kept getting worse. Her family didn't buy her any more antacid while they were there. She stayed at the San Angelo hospital with Leita until she got out of Intensive Care. She had found the Cowley's poison. It was high up and she had to tiptoe to get it. She was in the pantry cabinet to move some things around. The poison was out of Butch's reach, she said.

Lupton cross examined her and got her to repeat the schedule of events. This included coming to the Nobles home several times to take Butch to see Leita while she was in the hospital in Brownwood. Tim brought a plate of turkey to the house between the Brownwood and San Angelo hospital stays. She said a six-footer could see the rat poison. She said she opened a new bottle of antacid and took it to Leita, in contradiction to what Leita had said earlier. Leita kept antacid in the refrigerator because it stayed cold and that's the way she liked it.

Next on the stand was D. W. Shobles of San Angelo who met Olgie Nobles when he was in the pecan business about 1962. They were good, honest friends. He stayed with him at times after the accident at Leita's request. About March 9, 1988, he took Olgie to rehabilitation about noon to 2:30 P.M. while Leita was gone to see the doctor in Brownwood and as well as to take Butch to San Antonio. After rehab, Olgie could walk back into the house and D. W. said he went out to mow yards in three lots.

Olgie came out to sit on the front porch and watch. When D. W. got through, he said he noticed Olgie wasn't on the front porch. This was a little before 5:00 P.M. Tim's car was there. He went inside looking for them and didn't see them, but then Tim came out of Olgie's bedroom and into the kitchen. He started putting things away in a real hurry, Shobles related. Tim told Shobles that he had fed Olgie supper and gave him medicine. Olgie had already gone to bed.

D. W. said this was unusual as Olgie usually didn't eat that early and didn't go to bed that early. He had known Tim six or seven years. He met him at the air conditioning firm when he went there to get parts.

Under cross examination by Lupton, Shobles said he had mowed grass three times before Olgie's death. He didn't know about the girls who took care of the yard before then. Again the defense was trying to shift attention away from Scoggin. Weeds were about four-feet high. He stayed overnight one time. Lupton asked where the air conditioning firm was located, reiterating that it was close to the river with lots of trash and the building had a false floor.

Shobles said he remembered that at one time there had been a mother raccoon there with babies and some rats and once there was a lynx but it was a pet. However, most of that happened when the Nobles were in the pecan business some six or seven years ago.

John Poss, Jr., of San Angelo, an air conditioner and plumbing contractor, testified next, saying he had known Olgie Nobles for twenty years since he and Leita had bought out another person. They were friends and he worked out of their shop on a contract basis. He met Tim and worked for him. Gerald Hill now owns the firm and he works for him, too. Poss said he went to see Olgie every day he was in the hospital and so did Leita. He knew about Leita's ulcer problem as she always had antacid with her.

Poss said he saw Olgie a week before he died and Olgie was feeling good at that time. He didn't go to see Leita while she was in Brownwood and he thought she was gonna die at the San Angelo hospital. He changed the locks at the house as Leita was afraid somebody might get in after she found out she had been poisoned. This contradicted what Boss Sutton has said earlier about changing locks.

Leita didn't know what was going on around her while she was in the San Angelo hospital. He said he caught a possum at the business in a live trap in 1988 and a coon in 1985 or 1986.

Lupton picked up on the animal problem again during cross examination, going over the building diagram, false floor and trash and introduced pictures of the area. Poss was given power of attorney for Leita on July 25, 1988. He said Tim went to New Orleans and not Dallas as had been stated earlier for a china painting seminar. He didn't recall Leita coming in to help during that time as she had said. Poss said he tried to encourage Leita to go to a doctor and he believed Tim did the same thing.

Jerldine Barrett, San Angelo realtor and home builder, was a partner in ownership of the twelve-unit Sagebrush apartments in San Angelo with Tim. She said she had known Scoggin since 1981. He was manager of the Cactus Lane Mobile Home Park. He had told her he was an art student and studied all over Europe for a year before coming home to be a mortician and then he later got into the real estate business. He was associated with her in the apartment association and she sold him a number of properties. She knew the Nobles very casually.

She had lunch with Tim on August 16, 1988. Lupton interrupted to enter an objection at this point and the jury was sent out of the room. She gave additional testimony after the jury left the room. Lupton believed his objection might be prejudicial and irrelevant. She said Tim told her that Olgie's body had been exhumed and law enforcement officials were going to see if he (Nobles) had poisoned Mrs. Nobles. Tim told her that if Olgie had handled arsenic, it would be in him. Then they'd know he probably did it.

Lupton argued over the pertinence of this information and about Scoggin's knowledge of the exhumation. Charlotte Harris argued about this and said in her quiet, squeaky voice that she was going to ask Ms. Barrett about her opinion on Tim's business ability. Lupton said he would object to that.

The jury was brought back in and she repeated her testimony. When asked about her opinion on his business ability, Lupton objected and his objection was sustained.

On cross examination, Lupton attempted to establish that the exhumation and arsenic poisoning was common knowledge. Barrett said she remembered the exact date because Scoggin was arrested several days later.

After lunch, Mark Heinze, assistant cashier for eight

years at Citizen's State Bank in Miles, testified. He also serves as custodian of records for the bank. He testified that the Nobles had two accounts and a certificate of deposit. They did have three accounts in the first six months of 1988 and a CD. They started banking there in 1982. Signature cards were offered as evidence. On July 28, 1988, John Poss was added with power of attorney to signature cards. April and May 1988, bank statements on two accounts were entered into evidence. Counter checks were used, checks without names that for most of this century were maintained by many banks for the convenience of customers who didn't have their checks with them.

Heinze testified that in late July 1988, a check for $900 was sent back with an irregular signature as was a check a few days later in the amount of $2,700. He continued to stop checks after that. On August 3, 1988, Heinze said Scoggin and Attorney G. H. Lampley came into the bank with Lampley doing all the talking. Scoggin admitted he signed all the checks starting in May. When asked Mrs. Nobles' reaction to this, Heinze said he was told she was very sorrowful for what Scoggin had done. No money was lost to the Nobles account as it was covered by insurance.

Checks written in May included one for $7,700 to Central Bank North, one for $14,800 on May 23 to Nobles A/C, one for $6,000 on May 26 to South Glen (the apartment project in which Scoggin was involved), one for $3,000 on June 2 to Nobles A/C and others for amounts of $2,700, $1,500, $1,000, $1,100 and the $900 check.

Lisa Eddy, custodian of records and cashier and comptroller of Tom Green National Bank where Tim had accounts, read entries into Tim's accounts. Nobles checks were deposited into Scoggin's account.

Dean Feathers, credit manager and custodian of records for Central National Bank of San Angelo, said Tim along with Barrett had a $180,000 note on Sagebrush Apartments and Scoggin used one of the Nobles' checks to pay on the apartment note.

Texas Ranger Frasier was recalled to identify the Riopan bottle. He was asked by the defense to produce a picture taken at the Nobles home of a Tylenol bottle, which he did. This again went back to hints of possible product tampering raised by the defense several days earlier.

Leita Nobles was recalled to continue her interrupted testimony. She brought her glasses with her this time and was asked about braces on her arms. She said she was supposed to take them off and on every twenty minutes or so and take rehabilitation every day. She has not been able to do so during this week because of the trial.

Asked if she was wearing the braces for show, she answered with an emphatic "no." She said she never saw Tim put out any poison at the business. She also noted it was hard to describe the relationship between Tim and Olgie. Those were not her signatures on the checks she was shown. She couldn't write in July 1988. Tim had never made a payment on the $35,000 loan made in 1986 or 1987 by her husband for him to allegedly buy back the trailer park. She asked Tim once about it before her husband died and Tim told her he was working up papers on it and would start paying.

In tears, she recounted a visit by Scoggin to her bedside in the San Angelo hospital. "He came in and told me he was sorry that he'd given those checks on me, but he didn't poison me. He wanted me to stand good for them at the bank. I asked him why did you do this (write checks) on me and he said, 'I'm greedy'."

She said she told him to go to his daddy and work out something with the bank. Tim was not the only one who knew she had ulcers. She said she had a stepladder to get up on to get to the top shelf in the pantry. She said she kept staple food items there and didn't look up there but about once a week.

Tim told her that he didn't poison her. When asked by Harris if she poisoned her husband, she replied with an emphatic, "No." When asked if she poisoned herself, again she replied with an emphatic, "No."

Court was adjourned at 3:45 P.M. so the lawyers and judge could go over legal matters of "a very unusual nature," as the judge stated.

CHAPTER XIV

Trial — Day 4

The conference the judge and attorneys had the afternoon before turned out to be strange, indeed. It proved to be the turning point in the trial as to that point, the guilt or innocence of Tim Scoggin had been hanging in the balance.

Before the jury was brought in, the state and defense argued before the bench about the admission of extraneous offenses and testimony into the trial. Those items revolved around the death in Llano of Cordelia Norton, a $15,000 check to Scoggin from Olgie Nobles on March 24, 1988 and a $30,000 check on the estate of Catherine Norton. The defense objected strenuously, saying it would be prejudicial and in violation of Rule 404 of criminal evidence.

Judge Sutton ruled he would permit introduction of this information as it showed traits in allowable evidence. The defense said the prejudice was very large but Judge Sutton also ruled that the $15,000 check showed motive in the death of Olgie. He noted that all the previous checks allowed into evidence were written on Leita's account. Sutton warned the prosecution against allowing additional information in testimony. This resulted in numerous objections at the mention of various topics about the Norton estate.

Lupton proceeded to say he would object to all testimony, witnesses and evidence. He also moved for a mistrial on this. His motion was denied. He said it very softly and virtually inaudibly after the jury came into the courtroom. Sutton allowed his running objections and overruled them. With each witness and new piece of evidence, either Lupton or Edwards would object and this gave rise to puzzled looks on the face of the jury as they didn't know what was going on and didn't seem to understand.

Mark Heinze was recalled to the stand and testified that in a bank statement to the Nobles dated for the period March 29, 1988 to April 26, 1988, there were two withdrawals, one a counter check dated March 24, 1988 to Nobles A/C for $15,000 and signed by Olgie Nobles. He was asked about his conversation with Scoggins and Attorney G. H. Lampley concerning the amount of forgeries. Tim said it was $48,000 but the checks forged on Leita totalled only $33,100.

Lisa Eddy said that a $15,000 check was deposited into the Nobles A/C account by Tim on March 24. Also a $30,000 check drawn on Catherine Norton to South Glen was deposited and dated February 16, 1988, and the deposit slip was dated February 22, 1988.

Leita testified again, this time to say it was not Olgie's signature on the $15,000 check. She said he couldn't write on March 24 as he was too shaky and weak. On cross examination by Lupton, Leita said March 24 was the date Tim brought out medicine for Olgie.

Jeanette McPherson of Llano, a nurse at the Llano Hospital, testified she stayed with Cordelia Norton until the time of her death. She stayed with her at night and on some of her days off, roughly from 8:00 P.M. to 6:00 A.M. and 8:00 A.M. to 4:00 P.M. She did this for about two and one-half months. She had known Cordelia all of her life. She knows Tim and she said he had come to spend the night at the Norton home on several occasions. Cordelia died on Saturday evening, February 20, 1988. He was at the house on February 17 and left, but came back on the 18th and spent the night for several nights. He went to see Cordelia at the hospital every day. He helped prepare meals and took hot tea and ice cream to her before she was admitted to the hospital. Catherine and Cordelia ate what was prepared by Tim and the nurse ate some.

Cordelia became ill on Monday of that week and experienced vomiting and diarrhea. The doctor administered a shot. It didn't help so Nurse McPherson took her to the hospital on Thursday. After the death Saturday, Nell Summers, identified as a family friend of the Norton's, directed a meal that she fixed with Tim helping on that Sunday. When the meal was over, Tim asked everyone to come into the living room and told them they would have to leave due to the reading of the will with just he and Nell Summers present. Catherine had died on Friday morning.

On cross examination by Lupton, McPherson told of Cordelia's different health problems — she had a pacemaker, bronchitis. Cordelia had a number of pills but not as many as Lupton attempted to bring out in her testimony. If McPherson wasn't going to be there, she fixed up medicine for two or three days at a time. Cordelia had fallen in January and broken a bone. Lupton tried to get the nurse to estimate how many people came to visit but she said there weren't many.

She said Tim wrote a check on Cordelia's account to Jimmy Lee Ward for taking care of Cordelia's cattle although Cordelia said it could wait. This brought about a big objection as it showed Tim had written a check without permission. The jury was sent out and then brought back and told to disregard the statement.

Dr. Dan Hoerster of Llano, a medical doctor for thirty-five years who retired in August 1988, was Cordelia's doctor for twenty years. He said when she was admitted to the hospital, that she suffered from hallucinations, vomiting, diarrhea. He believed it to be a virus. He had never treated anyone for arsenic poisoning. He believed death to be due to pneumonia which caused congestive heart failure. With her medical condition, Hoerster said, arsenic would have caused these problems and death. He had treated her three or four months earlier for vomiting and diarrhea — about November 1987 — but it was not as severe as it was when she was admitted to the hospital.

Jim Sandell of Edgar Funeral Home in Burnet, was next on the stand. Arrangements for the Norton sisters were made over the telephone. He had known Cordelia about five to ten years through the flower shop. He said he told Tim that paperwork for cremation needed to be signed. He had known Tim when he worked for the Llano funeral home. Tim took the cremation forms and had them signed by Mary Moursand and Betty Graham. He was asked what a mortician knows, but he was interrupted by a defense objection and the objection was sustained.

After lunch, Roy Harper of Temple with Bellwood Memorial Park, testified that he has run the crematorium for six years and does cremations for a large area of Texas. On Monday, February 22, at 4:00 P.M., he performed the cremation on Cordelia Norton. It took four hours. It was the third one that day. The oven temperature swells to 3,500 degrees fahrenheit. No chemicals are used. Ashes were sent to the funeral home by registered mail.

Dan Edwards conferred with Scoggin before cross examination then asked about the process of getting ashes out of the oven, such as was it clean, etc., and he was assured by Harper that it was.

Johnny Waldrip, Texas Ranger from Llano, took the stand and told of his six years with the Rangers and twenty years overall with the Texas Department of Public Safety. He did the exhumation of Cordelia Norton's urn on September 11, 1988 and took the urns containing the ashes of Cordelia and Catherine Norton to the DPS lab in Austin the next day. On cross examination, Lupton asked about evidence gathered from the Norton home in Llano on September 8, 1988. Waldrip replied that the house was very clean. Lupton asked if he knew who was the last person in the house? Did he know for personal fact that Tim was the last one in the house, and Waldrip said no.

Mary Moursund then took the stand. She said she has been a Llano attorney for seven and one-half years and executress for the Norton estate. She knew Cordelia personally as well as a client. She met Tim for the first time on February 21, 1988 when he called her to meet him at the office to sign a form for cremation. The Norton will was signed for probate on February 25, 1988. Those present on the day after the death at the Norton home were Mary, her husband, L. T. Deschamps, Nell Summers, and Tim. She said that when it became apparent that Tim had knowledge of the estate, she asked him to make a list of assets. He asked her where the wills were and she told him they were at her office. Later he tried to "trick" her — then came another objection in mid-sentence and the jury was taken out again after the objection by Lupton.

Lupton, in the absence of the jury, raised the issue about reference to Catherine and also about the Rangers statement of exhuming urns. The jury was brought back in and Mrs. Moursund continued, saying that Tim asked if a person was a beneficiary, did they have the right to know. She said she told him she couldn't read the will at that time. When asked when, she said she didn't know. He was indignant and not pleased with the answer, Mrs. Moursund stated. He and Nell Summers met with her when the will was filed on February 25, 1988. She revealed to them the contents of the will. He and Nell were not beneficiaries. Scoggin seemed shocked and stunned. He was very quiet with nothing to say, unlike his previous behavior.

Later, Mrs. Moursund called him about the $30,000 check when she became aware of it on a bank statement. It was written on Texas American Bank in nearby Fredericksburg. It did not appear to be the signature of Catherine Norton, Moursund said. He told her that he had told Catherine he was having financial problems and needed money. He said she gave him the check. He said he told Catherine he'd pay it back at an unspecified time and at intervals. Moursund said she asked him why he didn't tell her about it when he was making a list of assets. He said he didn't think it was important.

On cross examination by Lupton, Moursund said she knew Summers was a friend but she just listened, didn't participate and there didn't appear to be any love lost between Summers and Tim. Summers was not available to testify as she had left the state and could not be located, according to the district attorney's office.

James League III of Fredericksburg, custodian of records for Texas American Bank, said the Nortons opened their account in January 1981. The check dated February 16, 1988, for $30,000 to South Glen was honored.

Carroll Bryle, Fredericksburg attorney for TAB, said he talked to Tim on May 11, 1988. He said he knew the date exactly because of a list he kept. He asked Tim how the check was issued and Tim told him he and Catherine were watching Olympics in the Norton home, talking about the past and Catherine said she wanted to reward him for helping them so much. She gave him the check. When asked if he signed the check, Tim told Bryle, no, that she did.

Ranger Frasier again took the stand to identify Catherine Norton's signature found in Tim Scoggin's home. League was recalled. Tim seemed to be upset at this point in the testimony. He had been more active this day than in previous days. League said the Norton account was not charged for the check as it was covered by insurance.

Scott Combast, a San Angelo pharmacist for Skaggs Alpha Beta for four years, identified the bottle of Riopan-Plus that had arsenic in it as having been purchased at his store. It was shipped from Ponca City, Oklahoma, warehouse in April 1988. The defense tried to imply the date could be a mistake but Combast said he didn't think so.

This piece of information was worked in by Prosecutor Smith as he wanted to destroy efforts by the defense to insinuate that the tainted antacid was purchased by Olgie Nobles in a plot to kill Leita. Since the bottle was shipped after his death, the defense's efforts to put questions into the minds of the jurors suffered another blow. The defense had hoped to make the jury believe Olgie might have been behind the attempt on his wife's life and inadvertently poisoned himself.

Court was recessed at 4:00 P.M. that Friday, a welcome relief for the defense as they needed the weekend to regroup and try to overcome the judge's ruling to allow extraneous evidence (information on the deaths in Llano of Cordelia and Catherine Norton) to be admitted.

CHAPTER XV

Trial — Day 5

The fifth day of testimony in the trial of Tim Scoggin saw a winding up of the state's case as they wrapped up loose ends. The defense presented their case in just a few hours.

First witness of the day was J. W. Zumwalt of Burnet, night manager for Edgar Funeral Home, who testified that he transported the body of Cordelia Norton to the crematorium in Temple.

Roy Ramiro of Llano, who works that city's cemetery, said he had known Cordelia for five years and was present when the urn containing her ashes was buried. The state was making sure that the chain of evidence was never broken.

Ranger Waldrip said he took the Norton check to the DPS lab on March 7, 1989, and gave it to Jerry Webb. He also took other documents with Norton signatures. Lupton on cross examination made it clear there was only one check involved.

Webb, a DPS forsenic document examiner for eleven years, examined the check. He testified there is no conscious thought given to a signature, although they can vary slightly. Signatures have pictorial agreement. On the bad check, he said, the uneven line quality called for conscious thought. You cannot use another person's signature to find out who signed it because of the conscious thought given to a trace.

On cross examination, Lupton asked about the signature of an older person who is ill. Webb said it can vary slightly with some variation due to loss of control, but its authenticity can be told.

Rod McCutcheon examined the ashes of Cordelia Norton. He received them on September 12, 1988, tested them a week later and sent some on to Dennis James at Texas A&M University. McCutcheon did three tests with the first two being inconclusive as the preparation wasn't right. The third test lasting about six hours showed 15.4 parts per million of arsenic. It was the first time he had ever done such tests and he said it was a high level of arsenic.

Ramiro was put back on the stand to identify the urn containing Cordelia's ashes. He noted that his "X" was on it. He had scratched the "X" on it out of curiousity to make sure the urn was genuine brass.

Waldrip was called back to identify the urn and the defense objected to it being introduced as evidence. The presence of the urn on the evidence table had an impact on the jury and audience.

The jury was sent out and the defense claimed the chain of evidence had been broken. Lupton stated that it was not shown how the ashes got from the crematorium's plastic bag into the urn. The judge agreed and upheld the objection.

Mike Roth now of Breckenridge, Texas, said he was Tim's loan officer at Tom Green National Bank and that Tim owed a $15,000 open ended note that he got behind on. He called him and found out that he would pay on it when "he got money from a trust fund that was being held until he was thirty-five." Tim paid the note in early February 1988. He had been given a sixty-day extension on the note which was to finance improvements at the Christmas Store.

Dennis James then reported on the results of his tests on Cordelia's ashes. Using a nuclear reactor and conducting his second such test, James reported that the ashes were separated into three parts, hard gray ash, dark, soft material and bone. He determined that the levels of arsenic were enough for arsenic poisoning.

After a two- and one-half hour lunch break, due to a

swearing in scheduled for the courtroom at noon, Gerald Pope, vice-president of the Tom Green National Bank, testified that Tim paid a $15,000 note on February 22, 1988, and also paid on a note for Nobles Hardware that he was several months behind on.

Jim Sandell of the Edgar Funeral Home in Burnet had been rushed back to San Angelo to confirm that he had placed Cordelia's ashes into the urn and had delivered the urn to the Llano cemetery for the funeral. Then since the chain of evidence had not been broken, the urn containing Cordelia's ashes was introduced as State's Exhibit No. 62. There sat the urn on the evidence table. The urn was obviously very heavy. It was almost like Cordelia was there to watch over the proceedings.

Jerldine Barrett was called back to the stand to be asked about her knowledge of the Norton estate. She said Tim told her he was good to them and he was in their will. She had visited in their home. He told her he was the executor of the estate and that he and Nell Summers would split well over $1 million in the estate.

At 2:43 P.M., the state rested their case.

The defense team promptly made a motion for instructed verdict of not guilty on murder and attempted murder charges as the state had not upheld the law and proven the cases. Judge Sutton denied the motion.

First witness for the defense was Becky Thompson of Midland who said she had known Tim for about three years. She and her sister have a Christmas store in Midland, similar to the one Tim had in San Angelo. Tim, Becky, and her sister entered into a three-year agreement to provide goods for Tim's store. They visited the store in late spring and early fall 1986. She mentioned about how rats and mice were a problem and talked about the condition of the buildings as had been mentioned in previous testimony. She told of how some of the merchandise had been chewed on. Holes were eaten in the ceiling. A slide show was put on by the defense with Becky making comments and there were pictures of varmint droppings. She also talked about junky conditions and made it sound like Tim had cleaned things up.

93

On cross examination, Prosecutor Smith pointed out that there was no telling how long the droppings had been there. Becky knew directions on everything involving the buildings as she had been well rehearsed for the testimony.

Tim Godfrey, chief of San Angelo Park Police, testified about varmint problems around the Concho River, problems with nutria, raccoons, red fox, squirrels, with the nutria being the biggest problem. Smith made him admit that nutria stay in or very close to the water. Lupton came back and got Godfrey to say that raccoons don't stay close to the water.

Next up was David Bledshoe, owner of a laundry and dry cleaners near the Nobles Air Conditioning business. He talked of varmint problems — he had trapped six or seven raccoons over the past few years.

Next on the witness stand was Bobbie Dindy, an elderly lady who worked at the federal courthouse in San Angelo. She had known Tim about seven years, having met him because his mobile home was on land adjoining land she owned and through friends who leased that land. She found out they had a common interest in china painting and starting getting together every Wednesday and Sunday nights. She patronized his store, especially the Christmas store. They went to seminars in Houston, two in Dallas and the International Convention in New Orleans. She said Tim treated Mrs. Nobles very nice, just like she treated him, just like you'd treat any little old lady. She didn't know Mrs. Nobles. She met Cordelia Norton one time as she had bummed a ride to Austin with Scoggin and they stopped by the Norton house and went out to dinner.

She said Tim and Cordelia had a real, real close relationship. They got along like they were mother and son. Cordelia became jealous of Bobbie. Tim would help them (the Norton sisters) out and send presents. One Christmas, Cordelia was in the hospital with pneumonia and he spent the time with her and almost forgot Christmas with his family. On cross examination, Smith made it clear that Dindy and Tim were close friends — there was a close friendship and real love between them. She said Tim and somebody else owned the trailer park and Tim managed it.

Dr. Michael Carlo, professor of chemistry at Angelo State

University in San Angelo for twenty years, said he was approached by the sheriff's office to do testing for arsenic but said he didn't have the equipment to do tests at that time, equipment he later acquired. He charges $85 an hour for his work and he "calls 'em like he sees 'em," he said, using an axiom from baseball. He went through procedures of how he had received the Riopan-Plus and the Cowley's Rat Poison from DPS. He set-up tests, performed by other people but all done according to his directions, to test arsenic, to test Riopan, to test Cowley's, to test arsenic in Riopan, to test Cowley's in Riopan and then the Riopan sent to him.

Based on his test results, he did not believe Cowley's sent to him was in the Riopan sent to him. He used charted samples of his ultra-violet spectography tests to show the differences. There was a peak in the chart that couldn't be explained. Yes, the Riopan had arsenic in it, he said. It appeared the jury was shocked by this. Under cross examination, Smith attempted to discredit Carlo's testimony. This testimony was damaging to the prosecution's chances. Smith asked if his test results could have been thrown off if something else had been added to the Cowley's and the Riopan. Carlo admitted that it could.

The defense rested its case at 5:00 P.M.

Judge Sutton called a recess until 9:00 A.M. the following day, telling the jury that the case could go to them as early as late Tuesday or early Wednesday. He said he would not send a case to a jury at the end of the day. He asked the defense if it wanted time for the accused to testify.

The defense team said they wanted to reserve that right.

95

CHAPTER XVI

Trial — Day 6

Tim Scoggin had three suits and he wore the third one for this climactic day. In the courtroom were his parents, his aunt and his sister, who had been in attendance while she was on a sabbatical from evangelistic work in South America.

It was time for the state to call rebuttal witnesses. First up was Irene Hutchins. She has lived in San Angelo since 1974 and was a secretary at Robert Massey Funeral Home where she met Tim. She and her husband owned Cactus Lane Mobile Home Park where he lived and worked as manager from 1979 to 1981. They sold it in 1981 for $500,000. Tim bought a small interest as he borrowed $6,000 from them and they signed a note for him at the bank for several thousand dollars. Tim is not currently a stockholder in the trailer park, she said.

She started to recount a conversation between Tim and herself but that was interrupted for a conference at the bench. Then the jury was taken out. Mrs. Hutchins proceeded to tell a story about Tim telling her about a book he was reading. He told her it was real exciting how a man used rat poison to kill people for money. He mentioned it to her more than once. She thought it was gruesome. That was the only book he ever mentioned to her. The judge did not allow her to repeat the story in front of the jury.

On cross examination, Lupton discovered that the money Scoggin had borrowed from her and her husband had been repaid.

Dr. James Garriott, chief toxicologist for the Bexar County medical examiner's office, was returned to the stand and testified about the outdated test that was testified about by Dr. Carlo for the defense and how unspecific it was. He noted that the dating of the arsenic and Riopan could have caused the extra curve in Dr. Carlo's test. There are newer and more specific instruments available. He went far but not far enough, Garriott said about Dr. Carlo. The additional peak in his graph about the anaylsis does not rule out anything.

On cross examination, Dan Edwards asked Garriott how long he looked at the graph — fifteen or twenty minutes? Where are your graphs?, Edwards questioned. There was an objection to this as Dan became angry. A conference followed at the bench. The judge in essence told Dan to cool it. Dan then asked in more subdued tones where Dr. Garriott's graphs were. He replied that he didn't have any as he didn't run any tests.

Garriott along with the next witness, Rod McCutcheon, who also had been on the stand before, were required to give their long list of references and educational qualifications.

McCutcheon then testified that further tests were needed on Carlo's theories. On cross examination, Edwards asked McCutcheon where his graphs were? McCutcheon had charts and the state tried to introduce them into evidence. However, following another lengthy conference at the bench, they were not allowed. The graphs showed arsenic was in the Riopan. At 9:55 A.M., the state rested its rebuttal. After a recess, the defense rested its case at 10:20 A.M. with no rebuttal witnesses.

After lunch, Judge Sutton read charges to the jury with definitions. The jury was very attentive. Scoggin never seemed to have looked at or even acknowledged the jury's presence during the entire trial. At 1:40 P.M., Charlotte Harris began the closing argument for the state, saying with friends like Tim Scoggin, who needs enemies. He wove a web of deceit and his greed led to murder and attempted murder. "We know he is a thief, a liar, greedy, willing to hurt friends. Lawyers' questions are not evidence." She went over the calendar of events. The jury was attentive, leaning forward in their chairs to hear every word.

"He confessed to theft," Harris said, "to take focus away from him. He stole $31,500 from Leita not counting checks totalling $7,200 which were stopped. He stole $15,000 from Olgie and $30,000 from the Nortons." Harris showed the years of experience of those who testified for the state, saying the defense would question the investigation. Scoggin's long term plan, Harris surmised, was that if Leita had died, he would have gotten away with everything. She concluded her closing statement at 2:10 P.M.

Steve Lupton started the defense's closing argument at 2:23 P.M. He thanked the jurors for their time and efforts to uphold the sixth amendment. He spoke eloquently about the constitution. Then he added that the state had failed to prove the case, their web is very confused. Where's the evidence? Web seemed very disorganized. There was no evidence. It's like a web — no weight, no substance. The jury didn't appear to be with him. Lupton continued, saying motive and opportunity is not enough to prove guilt.

The bottle is the smoking gun. Rat poison is the bullet but the bullet doesn't fit the gun. The defense witness (Dr. Carlo) was better than the state's experts. "What are we doing here," he asked. He talked about the confusion and how lawmen wore blinders. What about changing locks, what about the 7-Up bottle, he asked. He noted there was no surveillance or fingerprinting.

Lupton pointed to the Dindy testimony that showed Scoggin was a trustworthy, loving person. He continually raised questions and tried to create confusion, over Gober's connection with Olgie, the lawn girls theft, product tampering, the fact that the state didn't prove the Llano case, why lawmen didn't find rat poison earlier and again and again the varmint problem was dropped into the conversation. He closed the defense rebuttal at 3:26 P.M.

Smith gave the state's final closing at 3:27 P.M. He praised the jury for their dedication. He worked on straightening out confusion raised by the defense. Again the jury was very attentive. Using a chart, he tied common links to the case, arsenic and old people and Tim Scoggin. Then he ended by saying that "we all know who the varmint is here. It's not a coon or a possum, although he tried to play possum." Smith ended at 4:03 and the case went to the jury at 4:05.

The jury sent out three notes, one for evidence, one for some testimony and another for testimony right before they went to supper. The jury entered the courtroom at that point and discovered that confusion over testimony is not grounds to have the testimony read. It can only be read if there is a dispute. One juror had forgotten the date that Schobel last saw Olgie.

Those in the crowd who had been attending the trial, including those who were left holding the bag when Scoggin filed bankruptcy, speculated on how the jury would act. One man said he wasn't convinced of Scoggin's guilt until the Llano information was introduced.

Edwards was exhausted. It had been a difficult case for the defense as they spent many hours at work on it and got little sleep during the trial. He was glad the trial was over before the May issue of *Texas Monthly,* a popular statewide magazine, hit the street with an elaborate article on Scoggin. Before the jury came back, Edwards was talking to Scoggin's sister about an appeal and he said there weren't grounds. They obviously didn't have a good feeling about the outcome of the trial.

Just before going to supper at 7:00 P.M., the jury told the bailiff they had reached a verdict. They came back from a local, popular steak house, Zentner's Daughter, about 8:30 and sent a note to judge that a verdict had been reached. At 8:37, the jury foreperson told the judge that a verdict had been reached. Papers were presented to the judge who looked them over for a few minutes and then read the verdict on each case. To all three charges, murder, attempted murder and theft, the verdicts were guilty, guilty, guilty. As the verdicts were read, Scoggin was very ashen, his jaws tight. He never turned to acknowledge his family.

Scoggin's mother and sister broke out in tears. His father again proved to be the strength of the family.

Edwards asked for a poll of the jury. As each one was called on, they all said they were in agreement with the verdicts.

Judge Sutton ordered the jury to still not talk about the case and to return at 9:30 A.M. the next day for the punishment phase of the trial. He believed he would be able to give it to them after the lunch break.

It was a cloudy, cool West Texas evening as all this was taking place with clouds veiling what would have been another famously beautiful West Texas sunset. As the crowd dispersed that evening, the Scoggin family was shaken. They had so firmly believed in the innocence of their son, brother and nephew.

CHAPTER XVII

Trial — The Final Day

On this day that Tim Scoggin was to learn how much time he would have to spend in prison, court convened at 9:30 A.M. with no opening statements. The state introduced evidence that had been used during the trial. Dr. T. W. Carpenter was recalled to testify to Leita Nobles' paralysis. She said she was caused bodily harm.

The defense called Tim's father, Mackie Scoggin. In the audience was his mother, Billie Jo Scoggin, and his sister, Christi. She had been a missionary in South America and now teaches deaf children in Abilene, Texas, after having contracted a parasite in South America. She had plans to return to missionary work within the near future. She is not married and never had been and has no children. Mackie Scoggin recalled the family's life, where they had been and Tim's work and schooling. Mackie pleaded with the jury for lenience as his son had filed for a probated sentence and had never been convicted of any other felony. A short sentence could rehabilitate him just as well as a longer one.

Next up was Betsy Sadler, a niece of Mrs. Dindy who testified earlier in the trial. She is an early childhood consultant in a regional education center in Wall, near San Angelo. She has been involved in education for twenty-five years and involved in china painting which is how she met Tim. She testified that he was always courteous, pleasant and an excellent painter. He was always willing to help others. She asked that he be given a short sentence.

Tim always carried a yellow comb to keep his hair immaculately combed. The bailiff says he has been real quiet in the last few days and has been put under a twenty-four-hour surveillance since conviction due to his obvious depression. Court was recessed at 10:45 with the attorneys asking for thirty minutes each for closing statements. Court was reconvened at 12:30 for reading of the charges by the judge and sentence options which took forty minutes.

DA Smith did the closing statement for the state beginning at 1:10 P.M., stating that in making a determination of sentence, (the jury) must remember what came from the witness stand, remember deaths in Llano and then in March, the death of Olgie Nobles and the suffering of Leita Nobles. The jury was very attentive. Smith added that Leita may recover one day, but she was very near death. Olgie, of course, is gone, he said. Remember the forgeries all during this time, he urged and then told the jury to make a deadly weapon finding as arsenic is a deadly weapon. It was meant to kill Mrs. Nobles and it did kill Mr. Nobles, Smith said pointedly, then added that it was deliberate. He stopped the first half of his closing statement in five minutes.

Edwards did the closing for defense, noting that it had been a long trial, hard on everybody as it is an adversarial process. "We may have gotten a little testy and I apologize if we offended you." It's hard on the families, hard on Tim. "I never quarrel with a jury decision. The question is where do we go from here. We have to balance the needs of society and of this man," Edwards went on to say. Then he noted that there is not a likelihood that in this case you (the jury) would think probation is possible. Tim asked for lenience. "Standing before you here is humbling. There are different schools of thought. He's got some good qualities. We know the state's response to that as Tim didn't show leniency to Mr. and Mrs. Nobles. The maximum I don't think is an answer to his rehabilitation. I think Tim can be a productive member of society."

He urged the jury "to look deep in your hearts, do severe soul searching. Do the best for everybody including Tim." The defense closing lasted nine minutes.

On the second half of his closing, Smith said if you don't have punishment, you have a society of chaos. Tim must be prepared to answer for his acts and his acts alone. He belongs in the penitentiary. He has done nothing to deserve probation. What he has done is to deserve a life sentence for murder. He deserves twenty years for attempted murder and twenty years for what he took from Mrs. Nobles — the maximum fine and sentence on each one of these cases.

Smith went on to say that this was so sad as Tim had such a good background, such a good family. Then in a very strong, adamant voice and mannerisms, Smith urged the jury to give the maximum under the law as what Scoggin did, he did in a very heinous manner — what a dangerous man he is. The jury went out for deliberation at 1:30 P.M.

At 2:20, the jury returned with the maximum sentences in two of the three cases: Life and $10,000 fine for murder; twenty years and $10,000 fine for attempted murder, and ten years and $5,000 fine of theft plus court costs on each count. Judge Sutton made the formal sentencing after the jury was thanked and dismissed from their service. The jury found he acted with a deadly weapon, i.e., poison. This meant he will have to serve at least one-fourth of his life sentence, which is considered sixty years, before he is eligible for parole. That will come about in the year 2003 with good time credit for his time in jail before the trial.

Scoggin was told of his right to appeal, and of his right to counsel. If counsel was not available, it will be appointed. No bond was possible for sentences over ten years. All sentences are to run concurrent since all three charges were heard at the same trial.

There were seventy-five people on hand to hear the verdict.

103

CHAPTER XVIII

On to Llano

Tim Scoggin returned to Llano a depressed man following his conviction in San Angelo. However, the trip was not made before an attorney, San Angelo lawyer Tom Goff, was appointed to represent him on an appeal of the San Angelo conviction. Goff appealed the case on the legality of admission of evidence of extraneous offenses (the Llano case).

In the appeal, the contention was that District Judge John E. Sutton should not have allowed the jury to hear evidence in the death of Cordelia Norton and testimony regarding certain forged checks.

Meanwhile in Llano, residents were waiting anxiously for a chance to hear more about the case in Llano. Their appetite whetted by news reports of the San Angelo trial made the Llano public even more anxious to hear all the gory details of what happened to two of their prominent citizens, the Norton sisters.

District Attorney Sam Oatman was under pressure and criticism to get the trial underway, and for not having Scoggin indicted on capital murder charges. However, Oatman knew he didn't have a capital murder case. He had two deaths, one with motive and no evidence of murder in the death of Catherine Norton and one with evidence of murder but no motive.

Oatman was delighted that San Angelo had tried their case first. However, that also presented a problem in that he didn't know if the judge would allow evidence on a prior conviction to be allowed into evidence.

The judge in this case was Clayton Evans. Born in the small North Texas town of Munday on May 10, 1936, he attended the University of Texas in Austin where he also graduated from law school in 1967. Following that, he worked as an assistant district attorney in Fort Worth and went on into private practice in that city for a time before setting up a private practice in Burnet. In 1984, he was elected judge of the 33rd Judicial District for four counties — Burnet, Llano, San Saba and Blanco. He took office on January 1, 1985.

Sam Oatman, Jr., is a native of the area, having been born on July 16, 1941, and raised in Llano. He attended Texas A&M and then Texas Tech Law School in Lubbock. After graduation, he worked in the district attorney's office in Lubbock as well as in a private practice before moving back to Llano to join his father's law firm and become assistant district attorney. He was appointed to the DA's job following the resignation of his predecessor, Louis Crump in 1983. Oatman was elected in 1984 and took office January 1, 1985, the same time as did Judge Evans.

Oatman's right hand man is Investigator Henry Nolan, who lived his life in several Central and West Texas cities. He was born June 11, 1949, and attended Texas Tech. He went to work as a child protective services investigator for the Texas Department of Human Services in Burnet. He joined the DA's office in 1985.

On the defense team was Eddie Shell who was born in Bertram, a small eastern Burnet County town on December 11, 1950. He attended Navarro Junior College and the University of Texas in Austin then entered the coaching field. After coaching for several years in Big Spring and Seminole in West Texas, he went on to Antioch Law School in Washington, D.C., where he had a friend going to school. In the early 1980s, he moved to Burnet to join a law firm and then later went into private practice. He was later named public defender for Burnet County and served as a court appointed attorney for cases in other counties.

Assisting Shell was Paul DeCuir, a short, rotund man who was born in Nederland, Texas, on September 17, 1945. He was graduated from Lamar University and went on to law school at South Texas College of Law in Houston. Since being admitted to the bar, he has been practicing in the Beaumont-Houston area as well as in and around Burnet.

The first clash of these legal titans came in August 1989, only four months after Scoggin was convicted in San Angelo. His trial in Llano was scheduled for the first three weeks in December 1989.

Shell and DeCuir argued before Judge Evans that pre-trial publicity, plus the notoriety of the Norton sisters and small community gossip would make it impossible for Scoggin to get a fair trial. Shell suggested moving the trial to nearby Burnet or perhaps even further from Llano.

Oatman countered with the argument that information presented by Shell was not inflammatory, pervasive or prejudiced. The argument went back and forth, getting somewhat heated on occasion before Evans handed down his ruling.

"I deny the motion," Evans said. This was the first time for Evans to see Scoggin as the judge had suffered from a near fatal blood disorder that had incapacitated him for a number of months during which other pre-trial motions were heard. He continued, "The defense has not shown that publicity will create an unfair trial. I do not foreclose the possibility of moving (the trial) if publicity permeates the county during future hearings. I will not hesitate to transfer the trial. The question remains open."

Evans went on to give a gag order to all concerned in an effort to keep a lid on publicity that might require a change of venue. In Texas, judges are elected and Evans must have been keenly aware of the political ramifications of moving the trial away from Llano.

The Llano public wanted to see and hear everything about the trial. At the same time, there were pressures to keep down costs. Court appointed defense was costing $40 an hour plus expenses. Moving the trial would have meant extra expenses, and cost estimates on the trial were already more than what the district attorney had in his budget.

106

Following normal procedure, regular pre-trial hearings were held to make sure the defense was getting everything it needed under motions for discovery. With the holiday season approaching, it was decided to postpone the trial once more, this time with the trial set for early January. Then there were other delays.

With the 33rd Judicial District covering four counties, scheduling became a big factor, especially in finding several weeks to set aside for the trial. Finally that was done and the trial was set to begin May 21, 1990.

CHAPTER XIX

A Surprise

There was excitement in the air as cars converged and their occupants tried to find a parking space on the small town square around the county courthouse in Llano on that morning of May 21, 1990.

Llano residents were eager to see this sinister, cold-blooded man who was accused of killing two of their most prominent residents. Like many small towns, everybody is considered family even though they might feud and fight — but that was for insiders.

Outsiders, like Tim Scoggin, weren't welcome and they certainly weren't welcome to come in and do bodily harm to the "family," especially those who are prominent as were Catherine and Cordelia Norton.

The townspeople just couldn't believe that a person who was accused of doing this could be a small, diminutive person as they had heard Scoggin was. They had to see for themselves.

Many of those who came to get all the latest information to share with friends who were busy and couldn't come, were disappointed when they got to the courthouse. In the small, second-floor courtroom, there was no room for spectators that first day.

A big shock for Tim Scoggin as he waited in the courtroom for things to get underway was to see Charlotte Harris. She was the assistant district attorney in the San Angelo trial and here she was again as a special prosecutor assisting Sam Oatman.

A total of 300 people had been subpoenaed out of Llano County's 12,000 or so population. However, only about 125 showed up to pack the courtroom and line the halls and walls. An angry Judge Evans ordered Sheriff Gale Ligon to fine all no-shows $100 each. By time for lunch, that panel had been narrowed to some seventy people. Various questions were asked to try to weed out those who knew too much about the case and would not be potential jurors or those who had excuses not to serve on a jury.

Only four of the jury panel members responded when Judge Evans asked them to raise their hands if they had not heard or read about the case. About 11:15 A.M., a questionnaire was handed out and remaining members of the jury panel were asked to fill it out and return it to District Clerk Wanda Osburn by Monday afternoon. Then they were told they would be called back individually concerning when to return, beginning that afternoon.

As the first day stretched into the second day, court officials continued to interview potential jurors individually, in an effort to select a twelve-person, impartial jury. Scoggin was only being tried for the murder of Cordelia Norton. The murder charge for the death of Catherine Norton, as well as the forgery charge on the $30,000 check on Catherine, would be set for another time.

"We've got to take plenty of time to make sure we've got twelve, fair and impartial jurors," Judge Evans told the jury panel Tuesday morning. It took the rest of that day and most of Wednesday before enough potential jurors were identified and the actual jury selection process could begin.

Wednesday afternoon, prosecutors and defense attorneys quizzed the forty-one people remaining on the jury panel. They talked about various legal terms pertaining to the case. Oatman specified that the case depends on circumstantial evidence instead of direct evidence and that the law does not make a distinction between the two types of evidence.

"There is no eyeball witness in this case," Oatman pointed out, saying "we can't bring you a witness who saw this occur." Shell then added that jurors being individuals can reach different conclusions based on the same circumstantial evidence. "There are two sides to every story," Shell pointed out.

It was late on the third day of the jury selection process before the routine culminated with the selection of a six-man, six-woman jury. Oatman was puzzled and at the same time frustrated as he realized the defense had allowed the selection of friends of the district attorney and law enforcement. Even if he got a conviction, because of the make-up of the jury, it would probably be overturned on appeal, thereby calling for another trial.

Shell was playing his cards close to his chest. He knew he had a very winable case on his hands, but at the same time he wanted insurance for an appeal in the event the case was lost and a conviction handed down. There were a number of people who were acquainted with the Norton sisters and the Nobles in San Angelo. And those people had as much opportunity and as well as motives to kill the Nortons as did Scoggin.

Plus there were other suspicions and rumors in the case that Shell believed in his heart would put doubt on the case. None of those suspicions and rumors could be nailed down before the trial started and were still being worked on by DeCuir while Shell was working on jury selection.

In the meantime, there were conversations going on between the defense and prosecution on the possibility of a plea bargain. Oatman wanted a guilty plea in exchange for a sixty-year sentence for murder with a deadly weapon. Shell, DeCuir and Scoggin would not agree to that. It was the same thing as a life sentence in terms of how much time Scoggin would have to serve in prison. However, it would not cause any additional time because Scoggin was already under a life sentence from San Angelo.

What the defense and Scoggin had in their minds was that the San Angelo case was being appealed. No plea bargain could be considered unless the possibility of the San Angelo conviction being overturned was contemplated.

The prosecution came back with an offer of fifty-five years for murder with a deadly weapon. That too was rejected by Scoggin and his lawyers as the deadly weapon stipulation would require one-fourth of the sentence to be served. Scoggin didn't want to consider any guilty plea as he maintained his innocence and argued with Shell and DeCuir over the possibility of plea bargaining.

With the trial about to get underway, word spread like wildfire throughout the small community and a crowded courtroom awaited the opening gavel that Thursday morning. Scoggin as usual was groomed immaculately, wearing his tan suit and red tie. He had been in jail now for more than twenty months and the stress and strain of his anxieties and frustrations were obvious. He was nervous.

On opening statements, the rival attorneys tried to out good-old-boy each other and talk about the good and bad parts of the case and what they were going to try to prove. Oatman and Harris read statements from investigators and other witnesses that detailed testimony expected to surface during the trial.

Some of those scheduled to testify included people from whom Scoggin purchased both arsenic and strychnine poison for the supposed purpose of killing coyotes and raccoons. Others were expected to testify they saw Scoggin giving Cordelia Norton things to drink about the time she died.

Texas Ranger John Waldrip and other investigators involved in the exhumation of the women's ashes and having them tested by forensic experts also had given statements.

For the defense, an attorney was prepared to testify that Scoggin claimed he saw Cordelia Norton sign the $30,000 check written to his company, South Glen. This was contrary to what a Texas Department of Public Safety handwriting expert would have to say about the signature.

First to take the witness stand in the state vs. Timothy Glen Scoggin was Annie Lottie Wyckoff, a lifelong friend of the Nortons. She told about the illnesses suffered by the sisters and related how both seemed to be getting better right before their deaths.

She told of Scoggin taking Catherine Norton to Scott & White Clinic in Temple where she got a clean bill of health after having undergone surgery a month earlier. That was just two days before her death.

She said Cordelia Norton's health seemed to be improving when Wyckoff visited her on February 15, just five days before her death. Scoggin was helpful around the Norton house, making drinks for everyone, doing repairs, running errands, etc.

Following her testimony, the legal teams went into conference. It was at that time, that they worked out a plea bargain with Scoggin to plead guilty to all three charges, two counts of murder and forging a check on Catherine Norton in the amount of $30,000.

Scoggin didn't want to plead guilty but Shell convinced him it would be his best bet in the long run. The plea would be murder without a deadly weapon stipulation. In the event his San Angelo conviction was overturned, he would already have enough jail credit to be paroled, even though if the conviction was overturned, he would still have to stand trial again in San Angelo.

Plus, Scoggin was facing the possibility of getting another life sentence for murder with a deadly weapon that could extend his time in prison if the San Angelo conviction was upheld. Scoggin finally relented.

"It was so involved. We wanted to limit his (Scoggin's) exposure," Shell said.

When court was reconvened, Scoggin took the stand. When Oatman asked him if he had poisoned the women and forged the check, he answered in a voice so small that his "yes" could hardly be heard.

He was sentenced to two fifty-five-year terms to be served concurrently for the murders of Catherine (Girlie) Norton and Cordelia Norton and ten years for forging the $30,000 check.

The crowd on hand was disappointed. They had hoped to hear testimony that would give all the details in the case, information they now would never learn except through community gossip.

The plea bargain saved Llano County a lot of money, Oatman said.

CHAPTER XX

In Summation

Is Tim Scoggin guilty? Nobody really knows for sure except for him. All the evidence points in that direction but Scoggin insists on his innocence. Leita Nobles knows he is guilty.

If he is guilty, then he must surely be one of the most cold-hearted people in the world. Not only did he poison friends and those who trusted him, but he made them suffer.

It is not known for sure who was poisoned first, but it appears that Cordelia Norton and Leita Nobles were the first to be subjected to arsenic, based on their symptoms.

If Scoggin did this, when did he decide what route to take in dealing death to his benefactors, those who had taken him under their wings and helped him for so many years. Was the method he was going to use already in his mind from reading the book that he told Irene Hutchins about? Had he been thinking about it for all those years? Did the poisonings start after he bought the first Cowley's Rat and Mouse Poison in December? The first attempt on Cordelia's life apparently came before that, if she had been poisoned. It could have been that she was only sick.

There is no way to know how long Cordelia had been subjected to poison as her ashes revealed only that arsenic had been used to kill her. Was Catherine Norton killed or did she just die of natural causes? The circumstances are suspicious.

On the other hand, it is known that Olgie and Leita Nobles were subjected to a number of attempts on their lives over a period of months. It cannot be pinpointed when the poisoning started but it appears to be about the time the rat and mouse poison was purchased. Was that coincidental?

We do know that Tim Scoggin was a liar and a thief. But is he a killer? A jury of his peers thought so.

Epilogue

Timothy Glen Scoggin is now in prison in the Ferguson Unit of the Texas Department of Corrections at Huntsville, Texas, serving a life sentence from which he will be eligible for parole by the year 2003.

The only known, sole survivor of his intended victims, Leita Nobles, is slowly recovering from the attempt on her life. She has started a garden and still undergoes regular therapy. It is not known if or when she will fully recover from the affects of arsenic poisoning. The medical profession admittedly knows little about the recovery prospects of an arsenic poisoning victim. Few have survived and even fewer of the survivors knew that arsenic was what ailed them.

Charlotte Harris, the assistant prosecutor in Tom Green County, left the DA's office and joined the firm of Edwards & Lupton, Scoggin's defense attorneys, on March 1, 1991.

The San Angelo prosecutor, Stephen Smith, believes the case to be one of the most difficult cases he has ever been associated with in terms of establishing proof of guilt. The trial in Tom Green County cost the county between $50,000 and $75,000.

In the Llano case, the cost for the court appointed attorneys, Eddie Shell and Paul DeCuir, amounted to about $8,000.

The overriding question that still hangs over the case is what did Scoggin do with all the money he managed to attain? By some estimates, his ill gotten gains were in excess of the $1 million mark.

As a matter of interest, investigators attempted to figure this out. At one point, it was thought he might have a lavish, gay lifestyle. However, nothing could be proven or was even hinted at along those lines. Several people close to him have no doubt that he was gay while others question that conclusion. He is said to have never wasted a penny on personal items.

There were those who believed he might possibly have a cocaine habit. Again, there was no proof or even hint of this being the case. What happened to the money? One report has it that the money is in a Swiss bank account. Only Timothy Glen Scoggin knows.

Some three- and one-half years after the deaths of the Norton sisters, the estate has still not been settled. The Norton mansion was auctioned off for $165,000 in the fall of 1990, an amount that was extremely low but the real estate market was severely depressed in that area at the time. In the sale was some seventy acres where the building was located.

The City of Llano has received only $170,000 from the estate, money which it had to request from the executress, Mary Moursand, so that land could be purchased to expand the city's park, Robinson Park, the beneficiary of half of the estate.

One reason the settlement of the estate has yet to be finalized is that land in Llano as well as in Hawaii and Florida has yet to be sold. The urns of the sisters have been returned to the Norton graves in Llano.

Author Bio

Mac Bryton McKinnon has worked as a journalist since 1964 at all levels of the profession, working on a large daily paper, a semi-weekly, a weekly and a small daily as well as freelancing for various publications and preparation of several specialty publications.

A native of Dublin, Texas, he was born in Gorman, Texas, September 9, 1943, attended Tarleton State University in Stephenville, Texas, Texas Christian University in Fort Worth, Texas, and the University of Texas at Arlington, majoring in history with a minor in government.

He credits the success in his career to the many people he has worked with who have taken the time to share their talents with him. He started in journalism in the United States Air Force while stationed at Carswell Air Force Base in Fort Worth, then after completing his four years of service, worked at the *Fort Worth Star-Telegram* for five- and one-half years.

Due to the teaching, he received while in those formative years, he has been able to attain the dreams of most journalists including owning his own newspapers - the *Colorado City Record*, and the *Burnet Bulletin* and *Marble Falls Messenger*.

He then went on to be editor and publisher of the daily Pecos Enterprise, supervisor of the *Monahans News*, then moving to Colorado to be publisher of the daily *Fort Morgan Times*, supervisor of the *Brush News-Tribune* then he returned to his hometown of Dublin, Texas, in 2002 to own the *Dublin Citizen* which he sold in 2015 and retired. He has since filled in as publisher for other newspapers as well as continue to serve in a number of civic duties in his hometown. He has been nominated for the Pulitzer Prize five times.

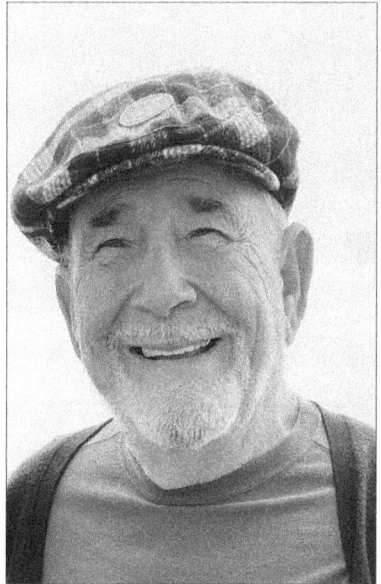